500 HOSTELS: AUSTRALIA
NEW ZEALAND & PACIFIC ISLANDS

Backpackers
& Flashpackers

Hardie Karges

ISBN: 0988490579

ISBN 13: 9780988490574

Library of Congress Control Number: 2013940653

Hypertravel Books,
Los Angeles, California

Table of Contents

Table of Contents

Table of Contents

Table of Contents

Preface: Hostels Are the New Normal

You better sit down, because what I'm about to tell you will blow your mind. We've got over two hundred hostels listed here in Australia, so for a population that barely passes twenty-two million, that's approximately one hostel for every 100,000 inhabitants. In other words, it's now normal. I suspect there are towns that have a hostel for accommodation, and little or nothing else. In New Zealand I'd be willing to bet on it. Sit down, I said. Here we have listed over a hundred hostels in New Zealand, right? The population is less than four-and-a-half million, so that's a hostel for every 40,000 inhabitants. That's huge! Now I should emphasize that while the following directory is fairly comprehensive, far more than the European versions, they are not absolutely so, so that the percentage might be slightly higher.

The comprehensiveness of the new editions is a notable change from the first European editions. I would say it's an improvement, but that's not necessarily so, not if you want to travel with a lightweight book. The concession I made previously was to limit the number of cities, and not so much the number of hostels per city, though that, too, especially where a hostel was new and I had no feedback from people who'd stayed there. I don't want to list a hostel "unvetted." So the new regions are much more comprehensively documented here. The only reason I didn't scour any deeper with Australia and New Zealand was to leave space for the other countries.

The oceanic countries ARE comprehensively listed, the big surprise here being Fiji. The almost fifty hostels here listed in a population of less than a million works out to a percentage of hostels to population higher even than New Zealand! Fiji is a special case, though, in that many of the 'hostels' are self-contained tourist compounds, so more reminiscent of Greece than 'flashpacking' Berlin. As with the North American edition I'll actually list the number of hostels per location here, since that number seems more definitive than it ever did before with my initial efforts in Europe.

Then there are large countries with very few hostels listed here, like Indonesia and the Phillipines. It's almost as if there were a line drawn on the map, or in the mass subconscious, on one side the enlightened modern states—with hostels—and on the other those still in darkness, with no hostels. On the island of Borneo, that's exactly the case. On the Indonesian side, there are none, zero, zip zilch nada. On the other side, in the Malaysian states of Sabah and Sarawak, it's hostel central, no doubt an influence from the Malaysian mainland peninsula, where they are also plentiful. I can't help but think that this is indeed a trend here to stay, perhaps a new "social medium," if I may be permitted the analogy. If this seems bizarre and a maybe frightening 'devolution' from high Western culture, remember that the YMCA has offered such services in the US since long ago, and into the present.

We live at a crucial point in world history, and if that seems to be loosely defined by high-tech gadgets, social media and increasingly antisocial behavior, then hopefully there is some meaning there somewhere. The more that people get lost in their virtual realities, the more that reality itself gets weirder. I think backpacking and hostels are a healthy response to this increasing polarization, allowing people from all over the world to meet in far-flung locations and exchange ideas and information, the same as is possible on FaceBook and Twitter on a good day.

I personally have some qualms and mixed emotions about "party hostels"—and I'm not alone—but efforts by some hostels to limit it by requiring an international passport is probably a reasonable and measured response. Most "real" backpackers like to party, too, of course, just not all the time. The real problem is not partying; the real problemn is security. To expose a careful traveler's most valuable possessions to the prying eyes of casual passersby is simply irresponsible. Some places even require an actual backpack—full-size—for admission, but I think that's going too far. I travel light. Still the existence of those party hostels is fairly predictable and well-documented. If you don't like it, you can switch hostels or switch cities, so simple. Australia has plenty to choose from, and much of it has never been "done" before. You won't be worried about getting away from the partiers in Sumatra. You'll be trying to find someone who speaks English.

The whole larger trend suggests a counter-point to the commonly held perception that people—especially young people—are retreating inward to their smart phones and their social media. Here in fact is confirmed in person and in the flesh the promise of that same social media, that you can have rewarding experiences with people "out there" — total strangers — and exchange something important in the process: information, advice, and most of all, good will. At a good hostel on a good day, you can do all of that and more. You can meet people of all ages and from all places, though you may not speak to your neighbor "back home" for a year or forever. Please read on.

Introduction

What is a hostel? Originally they were places, mostly in Europe, where students could sleep for cheap on extended country outings, frequently established at appropriate intervals over and about the landscape and which corresponded more or less to the amount of distance a student might hike or bike in the course of a day. Since those outings usually occurred in the summer when schools were otherwise uncommitted, the schools themselves became the logical place for seasonal conversion. That still happens sometimes, but not much. The concept has expanded dramatically over the last decade, for a variety of reasons, no doubt; among them: rising hotel prices, rising restaurant prices, and — drum roll here, please — Internet. For the rise of Internet has not only made advance booking widely accessible for both hostel and traveler, but it also became a reasonably-priced accommodation where a traveler would almost certainly have access to that same Internet. This fueled an explosion which is still happening to this day, and has barely scratched the surface yet in many places.

In the introduction to my book "Hypertravel: 100 Countries in 2 Years," I wrote, "Not surprisingly, hostels are least prevalent in places where cheap hotels and guest houses are most available, such as Southeast Asia." I just might have to return the Cuban cigar I received for that brilliant observation. At last count Singapore had over forty hostels, and even very-reasonably-priced Bangkok almost as many. In contrast Boston, in the good ol' US of A, has... what, two or three? I guess hostels, with their shared rooms, just aren't American. But all that's changing, especially in New York, with some of the highest hotel rates in the world. Even in Africa, especially southern Africa, the concept is huge and growing, and in Latin America, they're fairly abundant. The only problem is that there exists something of a flexible and locally-influenced definition of what really makes a good hostel, so that this guide to European hostels will reflect those considerations.

What any good hostel should have, by my own current standards, are: 1) cheap dorm beds, 2) English language, 3) a kitchen, 4) storage lockers, and 5) easy access to Internet. Of course within each of those categories there exists significant margin for deviation, but a place of lodging should make the effort to at least offer something in each of these five basic requirements in my humble opinion. Other things you can expect that probably wouldn't be considered "amenities" include DIY bedding (you know how to make a bed, right?) and the likely absence of a towel (though many have it, but charge). For purposes of this guide I had to decide what ultimately defines a hostel, and for me that's the shared rooms. It's nice, for me at least, if they have private rooms also, but if they don't have dorms, then they won't be in this book. This book is not intended to be comprehensive, so don't be surprised if you don't see your favorite party hostel in Brisbane. This book tries to be selective. There's a reason for that, several of them, in fact.

There are some downsides with hostels in general, though usually no more than the sometimes institutional nature of them. A bigger problem can be location, especially where they're rare. That hostel may be located far from the center and not obvious even when standing right in front of it, no sign of the business conducted within, many of them no doubt informal in their business approach. There are other issues, also, such as the once-standard curfews which are rapidly disappearing. Then there are the also-once-standard age limits, also in decline, though still there, the main problem being one of where to draw the line. I've seen upper limits anywhere between thirty-five and fifty-five. That's problematic for those of us who hold non-discrimination dearly *and who are already over fifty-five.*

Other hostels are more creative and limit ages only within dorm rooms. That sounds reasonable, especially given the other discrimination issue: most dorms are of mixed sexes, though female-only dorms are not uncommon. It's mostly cool and without problems, but still these are valid issues to consider. Most backpackers' hostels simply have no age limit, and that's the way it should be, I feel. Any problems can be dealt with on an individual basis. Another related problem is that in some cities of Australia hostel beds rank as decent long-term accommodations for some individuals and even families, who attempt to live there. Most hostels rightfully attempt to discourage this, as they should. Hostels are not transient hotels, after all. I try to weed those places out.

Introduction

It gets worse. Some small hostels are barely staffed, if at all, absentee landlords showing up to let you in and set you up, then disappearing until the next guest shows up. Some legitimate "boutique" hotels do that, too, where they rightfully value their own private lives, but others are merely renting a flat and calling it a hostel, with little regard to your needs or that of their neighbors. If you book in advance, and they demand to know your arrival time, then that's a good clue. If they call you in advance, that's another. If they have no website (the ones here do) and the hostel-booking site has few pictures, then that's another. Unfortunately a place with a bad rep can simply change its name and start all over as if nothing ever happened. I try to weed those places out of this guide and include only "real" hostels. With this guide you can contact hostels directly before committing any money, which is good. That way you can do some weeding, too, even at the last minute. You can't do that with most hostel-booking sites, which for some hostels is their only connection to potential customers.

For better or worse, consolidation is setting in to the hostel scene rapidly, and the days of the "hippie hostel" may be numbered. The most obvious manifestation of this trend is the appearance of hostel chains, not only within a city or country, but in multiple cities across a region. I think that this in general is good, as it establishes standards of services and expectations. The downside, that quirky little mom-and-pop operations may get squeezed out, is probably misplaced, since many of those places wouldn't rate very highly on my hostel-meter anyway, and the current "Air BnB" trend is probably more suitable to their offerings. Many of those would not even be found in this book, since they don't have websites. Conversely, many of the biggest chains will not be represented for every one of their branches here. I try to strike a balance between standards and individuality. Just because a place calls itself a hostel is not enough for me.

A word should be mentioned about HI, Hostelling International, which is often affiliated with YHA and such. This is the original hostel chain, and largely responsible for the existence of hostels, or at least their smooth transition from those early schoolboy barracks into modern backpackers' party hostels. They are a membership organization and you will need to pay an extra charge to stay there if youre not a member. When you've done this a half-dozen times or so, you'll be a member. But this guide is not about HI, though some are listed, particularly the ones that offer beds on the major hostel-booking sites. In fact they could probably fill a book larger than this of only their member hostels worldwide, though many of their branches are open only seasonally, so I won't concentrate much on them. For better or worse, they tend to represent the old school of "youth hostels" more than the modern era of "backpackers."

By the way in some quarters a hostel itself is known as a "backpackers," short for "backpackers' hostel," I assume. Make a note. Also, pricing gets elaborate and confusing, and frequently changing, so are included here for comparison purposes only. Just know that in Australia a dorm bed will likely run $20-50 and in New Zealand and the smaller countries somewhat less, maybe as little as half that. And for a private room, you'll have to pay that same price for two to three people, regardless of how many actually occupy the room. You should be aware that in some places—Melbourne comes to mind—you might do better price-wise for a small cramped private room in one of the chock-a-block centers of budget accommodation around the train station. That's when some of the other considerations come in, like Wi-Fi or a kitchen or...

The best thing about a hostel I've hardly even mentioned yet, because it's a hard thing to quantify, and that's the people you'll meet. Even an old geezer like me needs some social intercourse (yep) from time to time, and given our frequent differences from the locals, travelers are the next best thing. In out-of-the-way places like Tonga or Micronesia, that's priceless. In places like Sydney, that's "Party Time!" Don't forget to wear protection (for your ears, that is). So that's pretty much what hostels aka "backpackers" are all about. But what's a "flashpacker," you ask? I think that's what you become when you've been a backpacker too long and can't stop, maybe a little older, hopefully a little wiser, more up-scale and maybe less group-oriented, i.e. hard-core, or maybe 'die-hard.' I guess that's me. Some flashpackers may also be more urban and less interested in remote locations than in partying in the pubs. That's not me.

If you're American, then you're probably wondering why this historic trend seems to have skipped over the good ol' USA. Actually it didn't, really. Ever heard of the YMCA? They're always booked up in New York. This book's for you. America's indeed the last to get in on the modern trend, but I expect that to change very soon. I think many Americans just can't see themselves staying in dorms, but that's half the fun if you're young, and a surefire way to meet people. So what makes this book better than a website for booking hostels? That's like comparing apples and oranges. For one thing, we give you the hostel's own website and/or e-mail address and phone number for direct communication. So, not only can we be more objective than a booking site that receives a commission, but a booking site may show a hostel to be full when a call or e-mail to the hostel itself will get you a bed immediately. For another, we try to include only the "real" hostels, hopefully without bad reviews. But if they don't have dorms, then they won't be here, and likely the same result if they have no website.

This is intended as an introduction and complement to the vast online resources and hopefully a broader view. Still, hostel-booking sites are invaluable for feedback, specific information and special promotions, and I urge everyone to consult them. Two of the bigger ones that I know best are *www.hostelbookers.com* and *www.hostelworld.com*, though there are many others, and *www.hostelz.com* acts as something of a "kayak" for them all, so that's good. Then there's the membership-only *www.hihostels.com*, but as mentioned before, that's more likely an old-school "youth hostel," so not really the focus here, though some are included. If you're looking for something out in the countryside, they may even be best. But we're getting ahead of ourselves. This is a travel guide (both time and space), as well as a hostel guide. If you're a novice traveler, then you need to know some basics first.

Travel Basics & Traveling Around The Pacific

Transportation: Buses, Trains, & Planes

There's nothing more basic to travel than the actual transportation. In general that means buses, trains, and planes, right? Well, for international travel, especially inter-continental travel, that mostly means planes. But which planes? Well, you can just go to a travel agent and they'll be happy to do everything for you, but if you're a do-it-yourselfer like me, then you probably want a little bit more control over the process than that, and you probably wouldn't mind knowing how it works, so that you can tweak it to your own tastes and proclivities. The good news is that with online booking you can do that. I do things in the booking process I wouldn't dare ask an agent to do. The first thing to decide is where and when you want to go, and then start pricing.

First determine what's the nearest major hub city (usually the largest and the lowest price) in the region you're going to, or coming from, and then compare to that. Major hubs around the world include London, Paris, Cairo, Istanbul, Dubai, Johannesburg, Delhi, Bangkok, Singapore, Lima, and others. In the Pacific: Sydney, Auckland, Manila, Jakarta, Bali, Brisbane, Honolulu and Nadi, Fiji, are the biggies, in no certain order. If you're traveling abroad and want a multi-city route, then carefully check for airlines that hub in one of the cities on your route, for instance for LA-Paris-Cairo-LA, you'll definitely want to check Egyptair and Air France, in addition to a multi-line site or two. Expedia and the like can and will book any multi-segment flight on multiple airlines, very convenient!

Are you still with me? So what's next? In the old days I'd check the Sunday travel section in LA, New York, or San Fran papers—the library'd have them if the newsstands didn't—and start looking for deals from "bucket shops," i.e. consolidators. They'd buy large blocks of seats to re-sell and always undercut the airlines themselves, who were limited by IATA rules and regs in what they could do. Then I'd get on the 800# line and start chatting with someone with a thick accent in Times Square or Union Square or Chinatown or on Broadway downtown somewhere, trying to get the right price. It'd never be the price in the ad, of course, but I'd try to get close. Then I'd make payment and ticketing arrangements to be mailed back and forth, money order for them, paper ticket usually Fedexed to me, very "old school." Or if I were stopping in that same city on my way out of the country, then I might even stop in their office, if I could squeeze into the cramped spaces they typically occupied. Those ads have mostly disappeared.

It's easier than that now. Some of those places still exist—Flight Center and STA Travel come to mind as multi-city biggies—but rarely will they have better deals now than what you could find for yourself on the Net. I usually go to one of the major multi-airline travel sites like Expedia, Travelocity, etc. (or Kayak will pull them all up for you to compare) and see who flies where and when for how much. Then I'll go to the website of one or more of those airlines and compare prices. They're not always the same, and as often as not the multi-airline site will be cheaper, BUT... that might change tomorrow. The airline's own site will change less, but the multi-line sites can somehow magically splice together several airlines for multi-city itineraries, all at very reasonable prices. They also have hotels, too, but if you're reading this book, then that's probably not your thing. One advantage to Expedia, etc. is that prices include tax; with airlines' own sites, you'll probably have to continue to checkout to know the final price. Don't be fooled by false low numbers.

When to buy? You know that already, don't you? The sooner you buy, the better the price, right? Not necessarily. Of course you need to check as far in advance as possible just to budget yourself, but I'd say start checking prices seriously no later than three months before your anticipated travel date. But don't buy yet. Online sales are usually immediate, so you probably want to keep options open as long as you can. A travel agent might make a reservation for you and let you pay later, so that's one advantage to working with them. Then if you find it cheaper yourself, you can cancel with the agent or simply let it expire. Don't book the same flight as the one your agent's already booked, though. That gets messy.

I'd still advise you to do some legwork, regardless. If your dates are flexible, then check prices for each day a week before and after your preferred date; they'll probably vary, but Tuesday and Wednesday will usually be cheapest. Check again a week later; it goes fast when you get the hang of it. If prices start going up for Fridays then you might want to go ahead and purchase that Wednesday flight. If not, then wait. I've seen some major discounts right at two months out, if the seats aren't selling quickly enough, so wait until then if you can, fifty-nine days out if your plans are firm enough. If not then start monitoring every day or two. A large group can sell a flight out quickly. Once a seat is gone, they rarely come back. It's not like the old days when reservations were made, then frequently cancelled.

If you're trying to book a frequent-flyer flight from an airline, generally a tiered system will charge you a certain amount of miles for Europe (50K+/-), Asia (75K+/-), Africa (100K+/-), etc. without any advantage necessarily to the major hubs. Those hubs may have stiffer fees and taxes, too, and the award usually doesn't cover that. I'm searching flights to Africa from the US right now, hubbing out of Europe. It costs 40,000 frequent-flyer miles to fly to either London or Lisbon. London's fees are $600; Lisbon's are $200. Go figure. If you're using frequent-flyer miles attached to a major non-airline bank card, then usually now those convert to 1% of the cost of the flight, i.e. 50,000 miles = $500 flight, booking through their agent. Poke around the site first, though, and you might find a minor partner that still uses the old tier system (like Bank of America's Canadian partner). You'll likely get more that way if you're flexible with dates. Whew!

It might be worth a line or two about "free flights," the subject of more than one budget travel book, and a fairly simple deal. Deal is, usually, that you apply for an airline-based credit card, which will typically give you 30-50,000 free miles as incentive; all you have to do is spend probably $3-5000 within the first 3-5 months. Of course you have to have good credt, too. So it's a pretty good deal if you fit those circumstances, but of course, you can only do that a limited amount of times, and beware, the first year may be free of annual fees, but the second usually is not, and they can easily run up to $100 — or close to it. As long as you cancel the card before the fee is actually due, then you're probably okay, though, so check your bills carefully.

One more thing: not all free flights are so free. Beware excessive 'fees' that are not covered by your 'free' flight, especially on international flights. Some airlines charge up to $6-700 for that. Run a hypothetical free flight through the system before choosing that special credit card promotion with 40,000 free miles. Domestic flights are better.

The Pacific region poses some special problems for travel, seeing as it's an island region, e.g. there are few buses, except within individual countries, such as Australia and New Zealand. Also, it would be extremely hard to travel the entire region in one single trip, given the distances involved, but if you wanted to try, then the Phillippines, Australia, and Fiji would be the important hubs. The more northern Micronesia region is especially problematic, since it's pretty much just United Air serving the region, the milk run from Honolulu to Manila with stops in Marshall Islands and FSM the easiest—but not cheap—trick to fulfillment. Check both directions for best times and prices...seriously. Budget airlines in the region include Air Asia, Tiger, Pacific Blue, Jetstar, Webjet, and more.

Going the other direction from Honolulu, Fiji's Air Pacific has decent rates to Australia via Fiji, and if you can score a Bula Pass, then decent rates to Samoa, Tonga, and elsewhere from Fiji if you can fit them in your schedule. Once in Oz, you've got budget airlines, Phillippines, too. Usually Sydney is the main Australian hub, but for remote islands the northern ports might be better, like Darwin for Dili, and Brisbane for Port Moresby. Places like Nauru and Tuvalu have barely 10,000 people, so good luck there. They're on my list, too. Some places are served only once a week or so, so plan accordingly. Either Oz or Fiji, one if not both, should work as a hub. I doubt you'll find any budget hotels online there, though, much less hostels, though probably something cheap for locals doing government biz. Google hard, and maybe take a tent, just in case. Ha!

Visas: Consulates, Passports, & Letters of Introduction

Depending on your nationality and where you're going, you might need a visa, which is a stamp in your passport that is your permit to enter a specific country. They have to be applied for at an embassy or a consulate. Do that two to three months before travel, also, if possible. You already knew you needed a passport, right? Don't worry; it can usually all be done by mail, but allow plenty of time, and make sure your passport has at least six months of validity from the date you plan to enter the last country on your itinerary or they might not let you in. Visas can sometimes be picked up on the road, but get as many as you can in advance from your home, especially if you live in a major city that has embassies and consulates. Nothing is certain out there. There are companies that will do it for you, but it can get quite expensive. Google hard, but the best source for knowing what visas you'll need (if you're American) is probably *http://travel.state.gov*. Other countries have their own. If you're doing the work yourself, then check the websites of the countries whose visa you need to get instructions.

You'll need a visa for Papua NG, for sure, and it's not available on arrival, either. Of course, that's the least of your worries about Papua New Guinea. Strangely enough, Australia requires visas, too, even of US residents, but it can all be done online; better do it before you get to the airport, though. I forgot and almost waited too late. Oz is very strict about imports to its historically quarantined island environment, too, so even wood is taboo. Don't take any food. Check for the latest skinny on any visas for elsewhere.

Finally a word should be said about 'onward travel' or 'return ticket', which is frequently required for entry, to make sure you have future plans. This can be required as you board the plane, and as you enter the country itself. Generally if you have no plans, I'd advise buying a cheap ticket to the nearest neighboring country, then tossing it if you don't use it. There is currently scuttlebutt about creating a mock doc with an old ticket, but I don't recommend it. A fraud charge is much more difficult to deal with than a $50 Air Asia ticket from Medan to Kuala Lumpur.

Money: Currencies, Exchange Rates, and ATM's

Money is important when traveling, of course, the more the better, but you don't have to actually carry it all with you. In general I recommend ATM's, since traveler's checks are almost extinct, and you usually have to go into a bank to cash them, as opposed to the generally more available exchange booths. The problem with ATM's is that they aren't everywhere in the world, believe it or not, and service charges can be high. If you plan to travel a lot, it's worth getting a bank account that doesn't charge much for foreign transactions. You need cash, too, of course, and a credit card for emergencies, so I recommend a mix of them all, a few traveler's checks, too, if you've got them. You don't want to get stuck with extra foreign currency, though Euros or Pounds are not so bad since easily changeable almost everywhere. There's an art to using up your worthless currency. Buy gifts at the end of a trip to use up extra currency. The last few days change just what you need until you cross the next border. Small denomination dollars (or whatever your currency) are good for those border areas.

Change money at established locations unless you're desperate, and count your money carefully whether at an exchange house, at a bank, or on the street. But first look at the posted rates, both of them. There's a "buying" rate and a "selling" rate. Unless you're leaving the country and want dollars or Euros or whatever back, then the buying rate is the one you're getting, the lower of the two. If it's a good rate, then there should be no more than 2-3% difference between the two. If it's more than five I'd probably pass, unless I'm desperate. Also check to see if there are commissions or extra charges. In Western Europe there usually are. Use ATM's. Use any leftover currency immediately at the border or first stop of the new country you're entering, or you might be stuck with it. Some currencies are largely non-convertible, e.g. PNG *kina*. Use 'em up. Never exchange money at a US airport on the way out. It's a rip-off, same in West Europe. If I need to carry cash in US Dollars, then I usually prefer fifty-dollar-bills, since they'll get as good of a rate as hundreds, are usually prettier, and are easier to cash in a pinch. Old worn bills won't pass.

Most Pacific countries have their own currencies, but Marshall Islands uses USD and one or two down south use the Australian dollar, so those are the two best reserve currencies to be carrying, though unless you're Australian, you probably wouldn't want to buy any extra AUD these days. It's expensive, and they'll rip you off blind at the airport forex counters, too, no ATM's at the Gold Coast cheapo airline terminal, either. Clever, huh?

Communications: Cell-phones, Cards & Computers

I think this is where the phrase, "it's complicated," originates. If you're European or from most anywhere else in the world besides the US, then it's easier. But America is slow to get on the worldwide GSM digital network standard for cell phones, and that's what you need, that and a multi-band phone, one that can handle both 1900 (Am) and 1800 (rest of world) band frequencies. Most new phones will make the switch automatically; if not, then look in the menu for something like settings>network>band, and then choose the one you need. If you're already with AT&T, T-Mobile or another GSM network in the US, then your phone should work all around the world, albeit with high international roaming charges. You may need to activate 'world service' first. Poke around the website, though, and you might find some special arrangements for particular countries. Barring that, if you're going to be in any one country for very long, then it's worth buying a local SIM card and putting it in your phone.

What's a SIM card? Simply put: that little thumbnail-size circuit-board accessible through the back of the phone is your number and all the information that goes with it, including your calling history. It's easy to switch, but you'll probably have to "unlock" your phone first if it's American. American cell-phone services are traditionally monopolized, with prices to match. If that's what it takes to produce iPhones, then so be it. If you're switching services in the US, then request the company to unlock it. If you're tech-savvy, you might even find tools online to unlock it yourself. Otherwise, go to the sleazy part of town in some sleazy city (say, Sydney) where people do things they're not supposed to do and look for signs around cell-phone shops that say "phones unlocked," or something like that. Buy a local SIM card for ten or fifteen bucks, stick it in, and then start blabbing. Some might even be worth keeping, if they give you a better international rate than your US phone would.

Smart phones are too new for me to have the skinny worldwide. Buy the next edition, and I'll promise to be up-to-date by then. This is a real breakthrough, obviously, to have a local map in your hands constantly and ready to use. It's not that easy, though, not yet anyway. For one thing, there are the high roaming fees mentioned earlier. For another, the G3 system doesn't exist everywhere in the world yet, much less G4, so simply buying a new SIM card and sticking it in is not necessarily a quick easy solution. Stay tuned. As a lover of maps, I find this development exciting if only for that reason. After all, who do I want to call in most countries that I travel in? But maps are something else entirely. Of course using a phone with G3 internet to tether to your laptop is tantalizing, but not free. In many hostels WiFi is free.

Actually phone calling cards are still popular and useful, but you don't always need actual cards. Sometimes all you need are the PIN number and the access numbers, so you can do that online with much greater choice than in Chinatown. Ones that allow you to call all over the world from the US are dirt cheap. Cards that allow calling from anywhere to everywhere might be harder to find and more expensive. Read the fine print carefully. Of course even then you'll need a local phone to call the access number, so maybe not worth the hassle for a traveler.

The best option generally these days is to use Skype on your Internet device: anywhere everywhere cheap no hassle, all you need is WiFi for calling out or even receiving calls whenever you happen to be online. For someone to call you anywhere any time, though, you still need your own number. Skype rates may finally be climbing now, but there are copycats with similar services to compare to. As for Internet in general, Wi-Fi is an international standard, so available everywhere, of course, but don't expect them to be everywhere for free. Since you're reading this book, though, your odds are decent with the places listed here. One nice thing about G-4 cell-phone-style Internet is that it'll be everywhere there's phone service and quality should be comparable to WiFi. Then those GSM (GPRS) modems that connect to the USB port of your Internet device should truly be competitive with ADSL high-speed Internet. As with cell-phones if you're going to be around a while, it might be worth it to buy a local SIM for your GSM modem.

There is one new development regarding cellphones worth mentioning and that is the availability of "world phones," specifically intended for world travel, an option worth considering, especially for Americans, maybe even Europeans and others, particularly for those who need several different numbers for several different places. As mentioned before, most Americans don't have GSM phones, which is the world digital standard, and roaming's not cheap with ATT and T-Mobile, even if you do. Now you can buy a UK SIM card and/or phone and travel the world with a +44 number, and not only pay for the service in US dollars, but pay no monthly fees at all.

If you pay after each use, then the rate is no bargain, but if you pay in advance, then it's not so bad, comparable to top-up service in developed countries, some with the option to receive calls in many of the world's countries absolutely free, and especially good for West Europe if you're American, and vice-versa. It gets better. Many of these services offer the option of having two or more numbers available for use on the same SIM card, with some considerations as to which number is better for which countries, though generally it would be the "global" number for an American—usually a UK number, though I've also seen Belgian and Estonian ones.

Some services—particularly the Estonian—will even allow you to choose many numbers for use around the world, charges often only accruing if you need a permanent number. I've had a post-paid number for years for emergency world use, but now I have a pre-paid one, and so far it looks good. I may even use it for service in the US full-time. For someone who doesn't talk much, it's very economical to only pay for what I actually use, with no monthly fees, or only a dollar every two months to buy the number, and use the phone at least once or twice a year to keep the SIM card active. Some phones not only allow two numbers on one SIM card, but also accept two SIM cards simultaneously! How's that for service? Unfortunately most of them aren't smart-phones, boo hoo. Here's a website for more info: http://www.prepaidgsm.net/.

World roaming for cell-phones shouldn't be any special problems in most areas of the Pacific region, except maybe the tiny countries, but if you're looking for free WiFi, then be prepared for a shock. It's hard to find here. There's generally paid service available, though, so you won't have to go cold turkey. You'll just have to pay for it, generally in the form of pre-paid cards. Free WiFi is gradually creeping in and around, so if you find it, then you better grab it.

Security: Rip-offs, Scams and Insurance

Of course you need to be careful at all times when traveling. You're especially vulnerable when walking around with a full pack. Don't waste time in that situation; don't do it after dark; and don't even think about it in Port Moresby, or anywhere in Papua New Guinea, for that matter. And spread that money around, on your body, that is. Don't keep everything in one easy place. Losing a little is much better than losing a lot. Got a passport bag? Don't dangle it off your neck, either inside or out. Put your arm through it and conceal it snugly under your armpit, ready to be locked down tightly, with your arm. Carry that daypack in front or off your side; a thief in a group following you closely behind can riddle through your bag without you even knowing it. Be careful with strangers; maintain some distance. If anyone gets too close, or follows behind for too long, then stop! Let him pass.

Put that wallet in your front pocket; butts aren't so sensitive usually. Avoid crowds in general; but if you're in a crowd and feel a bump, then grab your bag or wallet immediately. You might feel someone else's hand there. That's how pickpockets work. Don't confront them; they're fast. You won't even be sure who it was. Tight passages are the same. Pickpockets wait there to pass through at the same time as you. Deal is: when you feel the bump, you won't feel the grab. If you're walking around after dark, consider carrying something gnarly in your hand, like an umbrella or a flashlight or a nasty-looking set of keys. A belt with heavy buckle that slides right out of the loops fast works well. Most thieves want to work quickly, but not all. There are slow scams and false fawning fraudulent friends, too. Remember to wear protection.

This is all for deterrence, remember; you never want to ever actually get into a tangle. If someone acts menacingly toward you and they're not yet close, then run like Hell. If they pull a gun or knife, then give them whatever they want. Your life is worth more than your iPad. In the unfortunate event that you do get robbed or mugged, don't panic. Go to the police, get a report, and start the work of canceling credit cards and getting a new passport. That means going to the nearest consulate or embassy and telling them you need an emergency termporary passport. They can usually do it in a few hours. If they imply otherwise, then talk to someone else. It can be done; I've done it. Hopefully you've got a copy of the passport; that helps. A birth certificate also helps. Remember to allow extra time at the airport of your departure, as they'll need to fix the entry stamp that's now in your lost passport. Hopefully you've got a few bucks stashed away. That helps. Don't be shy about asking for help. Get religion; that helps.

Political security is another consideration, and for an American the most thorough update is from the site already mentioned: *http://travel.state.gov,* then divide by half and that's about right (they're more cautious than your mama). Keeping up with the news is a good idea, especially for the countries where you're going. Last decade's war zones can be great travel bargains, though, like Belfast, Belgrade, Beirut, and… give Baghdad some more time. Simply put: be careful and don't take chances. An ounce of prevention is worth a kilo of cure.

I'm not a big insurance guy, considering it in general to be a rip-off, but others have differing opinions. If you're booking a flight on a multi-line booking site, it'll be available there, sometimes on individual airlines' websites also. Some promote it heavily to pad the bill; you might have to opt out to get it off the bill. If you're going somewhere dangerous, that ups the ante a bit, of course.

Security is a problem in some areas of the Pacific, so better check current warnings with the US State Department as mentioned above. Papua New Guinea is a major concern, and I really can't recommend independent travel there, to be honest. It's a shame, too, because it's a beautiful culture, but that's the current situation. Hopefully it will change; I've seen it happen before elsewhere. The Solomon Islands is similar culturally—but without all the incredible folk art—still, a safer substitute. I wouldn't get any false sense of security there, though, either. There's a reason Honiara doesn't look like much. The locals burnt down all the Chinese shops a few years ago. There are no hostels there, anyway, not really, though there's something similar halfway up the hill above town, mostly local, run by an Anglican brother. Wanna' go native?

Manila, Phillippines, requires some extra caution; street urchins are the best pickpockets in the world, plus the entire nation has a rep for being more violent than the typical SE Asian country, with which it is very similar otherwise. And there are some urban areas in Indonesia probably best avoided. I was strenuously warned not to walk through the Arab quarter of Surabaya. Sometimes you don't ask why. You just obey: word to the wise, etc. Don't be fooled by the romantic images of mile-wide smiles, grass skirts and gently waving palm fronds, either. Parts of the Pacific are some of the wildest places on Earth, especially where alcohol is replacing kava as the drug of choice; especially where people are poor and foreigners make easy targets. I've heard bad things about Chuuk (Truk) in FSM, while next door in Pohnpei there is no problem whatsoever. Google for latest updates.

Health: Vaccinations, Food and Drugs

You know the drill, right? Multiple rounds of shots wherever you go and for the tropics, don't forget the prophylaxis, right? To be honest, I've never gotten most of those shots, just the ones required by law, but it would be irresponsible of me to suggest that you do the same. Tropical areas are certainly the problem, so require extra caution, though yellow fever is usually the only shot actually required by law. If you have to get that in the US just to get a visa, then it'll set you back a cool $100-150. If you can get it on the road somewhere, then it might be as little as ten bucks. Ask at public health centers; sometimes they'll jab you right at the border, just to facilitate matters. Some vaccines seem not much better than the disease, so use your judgment. Malaria prophylaxis is easy enough if you're actually entering a malarial area, but so are mosquito nets. Don't ever have sex with locals without a condom.

If the food seems strange at first wherever you happen to be, then go slow with it, allow your bacteria some time to adapt. You should experiment, though, since some of the local delicacies are delicious. Just make sure that foods have been recently made and are best served hot. The nose knows. Ask locally about water quality, though it's usually easy enough to drink bottled water or boil tap water first to be sure.

As for recreational drugs, I've got a simple rule: nothing never no way no how—just kidding! But you should be aware of the risks. A lot of countries take simple possession of marijuana as a *very serious offense*, punishable by death, or you might wish you're dead by the end of it. I would not advise traveling with ganja anywhere in the world. That smell is hard to get out. If you just gotta' have a little smoke once in a while, then I advise you to befriend the hipsters wherever you end up, which carries its own set of risks. Better yet, why not just quit for a while? You might be amazed how much easier you catch that buzz when you get home. It's the contrast that counts. Being stoned all the time is no fun. Of course more and more countries are legalizing it, so that's good. Latin America may soon be a dope-friendly continent, what with Uruguay already legal and others considering it, most of them tolerant, Europe too. Asia is intolerant.

Unfortunately more and more Muslim countries are outlawing alcohol, so it's the same thing. Take a break; you'll enjoy it more if/when you start back. Many Muslim-lite countries are growing more fundamentalist. Your best bet there are hotels, which are often considered international zones exempt from local standards. Remember that wherever you are, especially poor countries, that as a rich (yes) foreigner, you're vulnerable, so be careful. If you've just got to get a buzz once in a while, you might consider checking out the pharmacies. Things are legal overseas that are controlled tightly in the US; be creative, and read instructions carefully. It might be a good time to fix that cough. The cough syrup overseas is excellent. Check the ingredients. It even cures coughs... sometimes.

If you've got a serious drug habit, then you really should de-tox. It doesn't go well with travel. You should be careful even when drinking with locals. Mickeys do get slipped, and so do roofies. Finish that drink before going to the head. Don't accept drinks already opened, in bars or buses or trains, whether alcohol, milk or water. It's better to offend than to get robbed. Let me be clear that I do not advocate any drug use myself (I rarely if ever even drink now) but I understand the desire, so wish to see it done responsibly. But if you think you'll stay in hostels because those sound like cool places to smoke pot, then think again. I've never — I repeat, **never** — seen so much as a joint smoked at a hostel. Alcohol, yes, that's fairly common in hostels, but not pot.

Health concerns in the Pacific are typical of the tropics, so you need to check individual locations for particular problems. Certainly in parts of Indonesia and the Phillippines, you'll be in the over-populated rural tropics, so be careful of what you eat and drink. If you like those *nasi padang* stalls in Indonesia where the curries sit out all day, then the earlier the better of course. *Kava* is the traditional drink of the region, something of a stimulant, and rather pleasant if you can swallow the taste (pun), but beware the water. Even better is the traditional ritual that usually surrounds it, a social circle of music, communion, and ritual kava drinking. In some places, it's sold pre-mixed, bottled and iced, but usually it's mixed up and imbibed on the spot. In American Samoa, you can buy the dry powder packaged and ready to carry back stateside. Or they have US Post Offices there, too.

Recreational drug use varies by region, particularly in regard to cannabis. Indonesia and Malaysia are certainly not places to press your luck, Phillippines either, while in New Zealand a cop would probably ask you to share. They and Oz have the highest rates of cannabis use in the world, and I suspect are no more than a couple of referenda behind the rest of us in ultimately legalizing it, for medicinal use, if nothing else. You might run across some locals with something like a pan-island Rastafarian sentiment, as if island life carried the cultural DNA for stoniness, so you know those guys have the good stuff. Be careful, though. Hawaii's got the fabled "Maui wowie," of course, and the US territory of Marianas is decriminalizing, so those are safer options for island toking. This ain't Jamaica. Pharmaceuticals are safer if you just need a non-alkie buzz, no stigma attached.

Cultural Considerations: Sex, Religion and Politics

Among Western or westernized countries it's no big deal, of course. Our informality is our calling card and our stock in trade. That's not true elsewhere, though it's tricky to intuit. Some of the rockingest whoringest countries can be quite conservative amongst locals, Thailand for instance. In Thailand you'll rarely see locals kissing in public, though in the international zone, you'll see much more than that, of course. Vietnam has no such taboo, and couples hang all over each other in parks. Act conservatively until you know the local mores. As corny as it sounds, we are ambassadors to the world, and I'd like to think we have a larger mission to bring people together through our highest common denominators.

Think hard before taking on a local girlfriend, a good girl, that is. It'll take some time and patience. Women won't have such a problem, but just be warned that many local guys will only want a quick fling with a wild Western woman. If and when it comes time to do the nasty, always keep a few millimeters between you and the object of your affection. Anything else would be the ultimate in foolishness. Politics is always a bit dicey to discuss in public unless you know your host and his or her inclinations. Some places there can even be legal repercussions, such as Communist countries and a few Muslim ones. Tone it down. Most cultural considerations usually boil down to something much more mundane, though. Shoes are customarily removed when entering houses, and sometimes buildings, in much of the world, whether Buddhist, Hindu, or Muslim, so please comply willingly. They take it seriously.

In the Pacific region, Indonesia, Brunei and Malaysia are Muslim, so those considerations apply: keep your clothes on, and take your shoes off. If anybody tells you that Malaysian girls like to party, then he's talking about ethnic-Chinese Malaysians; that's different. Actually people are fairly conservative throughout the region, so act accordingly. The word *taboo* is Polynesian. Most of the region is Christian, and some quite seriously, so things can really shut down on Sunday. It's kinda fun to go church-hopping, actually, and fairly easy, too, just hang out in front of the door and see who's got the best music. If you're thinking maybe you'll bag an island girl or two, though, you better think twice. Some of those Polynesian girls are HUGE, for one thing. There's plenty of prostitution in the Phillippines, of course. Manila's full of it, a major sex-tourism destination. Cool bars where locals and foreigners can meet and mix are unfortunately not that common, though Tonga might be the exception. Oz and New Zealand party all night, of course. Guam's interesting, island ambience with Japanese food and British pubs... but no hostels, not yet, anyway. Give 'em a year or two.

What to Pack: Clothes, Communications and Cosmetics

There's one simple rule: travel light. I personally carry a day-pack and a laptop computer bag only, no matter the destination, no matter the length of the trip. Forget the monopoly board; forget the five-pound toilet kit; and most of all: forget the library (including all those 500-page travel guides), except for this book, of course. A laptop or Nook or Kindle can hold all the books you'll ever need *or you can buy whatever you need whenever you need it.* That is true of almost everything. A few changes of clothing are all you need, and a change of shoes, preferably a variety of things that can be layered as needed. The trick is to wash clothes as you go along, every chance you get, very easy if you have a private room with sink, not so easy in a dorm, but they frequently have machines there, so do everything up whenever you get the chance, except the set you're wearing.

Wear those hiking boots when you actually travel, so you never have to pack them. Add a pair of flipflops or kung fu slippers or sneakers to that, and you're set. My secret item is a down padded vest, which will compress to almost nothing, and keep you very warm in the coldest situations (plus cushion your pack and be a bus pillow and...). Add a long-sleeve shirt, and a T-shirt or two, which can go under or alone, a couple flowery shirts to accompany those pheromones you'll be sending to the opposite sex, a pair of long pants, a pair of shorts and a pair for swimming, and you're set. Use small 100ml bottles for toiletries (per carry-on restrictions), a needle and thread, a small umbrella, a power adaptor for multiple countries (and dorm rooms with few sockets), a luggage lock, and... That's about it. Don't forget the Internet device.

Except for the southern reaches of Australia and New Zealand, and a few high peaks, the Pacific region is pretty uniformly warm and tropical. It shouldn't require much heavy clothing. You'll want a rain poncho, though, and don't forget your rubbers. Local land transport does not favor a large pack. Travel light.

Travel Guides: Books, Maps and Internet

Guidebooks and Internet should work together for travel, but I think the relative importance is reversed. Instead of carrying a big book around for your basic travel information and then using Internet to book hostels and play around on FaceBook, I suggest using Internet for basic travel information, too. Not only is the amount of information enormous, but it's updated constantly. This book can help finding hostels, too, whether you have Internet or not. For me large travel guides are not only an anachronism, but were never really necessary in the first place, maybe to read up on beforehand, but not to travel with. I've rarely traveled with one. Most travel is largely intuitive, and a book removes you from that. I would recommend it only in the most remote or linguistically-challenging places, when it might really aid survival.

One thing I DO like to travel with are maps. But they're cumbersome, hard to find and harder to handle. Once again Internet is perfect for this, every place in the world available from multiple views. The Internet links I've provided here all contain maps within their sites, though a simple Google search is easy enough. I look at maps the way some people look at pornography; I can't get enough of them. One of the main problems with hostels, of course, is that they're hard to find, so that you almost need detailed destructions at some point regardless. I'm hoping that this guide can help bring hostels into the mainstream and promote some standardization. There will always be local and regional quirks as to how they operate. This is a book to carry with you.

How Hostels Work

But for a few small differences, a hostel works the same as any hotel, guesthouse, lodge, B&B, whatever. I won't insult your intelligence by explaining to you that basically you're paying for a place to sleep. Where it differs mostly from the others is that at a hostel you'll likely be sharing your room with a bunch of others in similar bunk beds. That creates a unique set of circumstances which requires some attention to detail. First there's the booking process. If you're staying in a dorm, then often you'll have to decide how many roommates you want. The more roommates you have, the less the price generally.

Hostels are generally booked in advance; otherwise they can be hard to find. That's once reason this book exists, to help with last-minute walk-ups and walk-ins. That's very possible in much of Europe where hostels are properly signed and conveniently located. Call first if it's a long walk or ride. I never made an advance room reservation in twenty-five years. It's nice to be spontaneous. This way you can look at it first, too, never a bad idea if you've got the time. Don't do that around midnight. Advance booking might still be cheaper, and hostel-booking sites may be cheaper than the hostel's own website. Shop and compare. If you book in advance you'll probably need to pay a deposit in advance by credit or debit card, usually 10%. Upon arrival, you'll need to pay the rest. I'll try to tell you here which take plastic, but don't count on it. Carry enough cash, just in case. If you want extra days, advise in advance if possible. For a long stay, you might want to book two or three places two or three days at the time if you don't know them well. That way, if you get a bad one, then you'll be out soon.

Obviously there is an inherent security situation with hostels that needs addressing and some malcontents seem to have figured out the basic equation faster than those in charge. I mean… I hate to be a spoilsport, here, but just because somebody stays in a hostel doesn't mean he's honest and loyal. I don't know about you, but that's my life there in that backpack, and I'm hesitant to just toss it there on the floor and walk out assuming it's secure. That's why every hostel needs lockers, and you need a lock. Lockers don't always have them, and if there are no lockers, then try to lock your pack directly to the metal frame of the bed or something similar. No thief wants to jimmy a lock if he doesn't have to; he'll take what's easiest. If you're in the room with others, don't show a lot of valuables; the walls have eyes.

Curfews are largely a thing of the past, except in the original "youth hostels," but beware the mid-day lockout, which some places impose "for cleaning," though you and I both know they're just saving on employee costs, maybe the entire profit margin at a small place. There's a good side to that, of course: the place is secure while you're out. Conversely, since the demise of the curfew, hostels have become popular places to party, sometimes facilitated by the hostel management themselves (beware in Sydney, or Tallinn, or London, or...). If the kitchen is full of liquor bottles, then that's a good sign. If there are hordes of Homies, i.e.local non-travelers, hanging out, then that's another. The yobs coming in to London from Hounslow for the weekend tend to look and act differently than the travelers from the Continent. Another sure sign is when a hostel has its own in-house bar. I'll try to tell you here when that's the case, but read the signs at check-in also.

As already mentioned, if it's a real hostel, it should have a kitchen for your use. That's nice, especially if there are no eateries nearby. Breakfast is less important, for me at least, though coffee and tea are certainly nice. So first thing I do upon arrival is stock up on food. If you wait too long, then there's no need. I tend to carry a few basics with me, so that's a start. Having a fridge is the most important thing. It's best to keep all your things in one bag and date and mark it as yours. Check the freebies bin if you're short of something. Don't take other people's food. Ask first. Most hostel people really ARE nice.

How This Book Works

How this book works is really simple. I've given you names, addresses, and phone numbers, everything but latitude and longitude, of the hostels included, so all you have to do is find the place. I advise to call ahead if you have no reservation. And I still advise booking ahead when possible, even when it's just two or three days away, so I've included website URL's, too. Many of those have contact forms within them. I've included e-mail addresses elsewhere. If you go from hostel to hostel, then you'll usually have Internet. Where this book comes in really handy is when that link is broken and you need to find a hostel when Internet is not readily available. Invariably somewhere the Internet will be down.

Of course it's the options that constitute the decision-making process in choosing a hostel, so in this guide all are listed for the following: Kitchen (or not), Breakfast (free or not or for purchase only), Wi-Fi (free or not or for purchase only), Private rooms (available or not), Lockers (available or not), and office hours. Most of this is common sense and easily understood, but a few categories may require explanation, e.g. private rooms. Hostels may be defined by their dorm beds, but for some of us, that's not optimal. I'm a light sleeper and don't appreciate being awoken in the middle of the night. Frequently I'll pay up to double to have my own room, and even then will usually come out ahead of a hotel. Nevertheless a place that has no dorms is not a hostel in my dictionary, so it's good to have both. But if you book a private room at a hostel, don't expect the same quality as a five-star hotel, or even a one-star. It's basic, but it's yours. And you might have to pay a pretty penny for that Wi-Fi elsewhere.

Lockers are fairly rare, actually, especially considering the security risk in an open dorm. Go figure. Thefts are rising. Costs are for comparison only and are something of an average, a price actually offered at a non-peak/non-slow time of year. There are always promotions and seasonal changes and varying specifications, so check around. A hostel-booking site might be cheaper than the hostel's own site. Some hostels have free WiFi; some charge; some have none, same with computers. Contact the hostel directly if the information here is insufficient. If you don't like using a credit card online, then contact the hostel and see if other arrangements are possible. Some require full payment in advance during special seasons. There are many hostel chains now, and I may not list them all in the same town. Check their website. Most of these hostels have websites or I won't list them. Information here can be wrong. Check their website.

This book is intentionally intended to be part of a paradigm shift toward a new era in budget travel. If the old paradigm of the backpacker walking down the street with huge guidebook in hand trying to find budget accommodation is already out-of-date, then I think the one of booking them all in advance is not much better. There needs to be a balance of advance planning and spontaneity, guidebook and Internet. That's already the case, of course; I only propose to shift the balance toward less book and more Internet. This book is designed for that purpose. Not only do I hope to make hostelling better for backpackers, but I hope to see more hostels enter the mainstream, with better signage, better facilities, and ultimately more customers.

You might notice that addresses and phone numbers, everything but Internet addresses, are listed in several different ways. That's both accidental and intentional, accidental in that I tend to leave them as they're given to me, intentional in that you'll see them many ways, so this prepares you to adapt. With phone numbers generally "+" precedes an international number. With a cell phone, hold the "0" down and "+" will appear. That saves you from having to know codes *for international calling* (011, 001, etc.) in every country. That same number used within the country would usually drop the "+" and the 2-3 number code following it and add a "0" at the front. Compare them and you'll see. A picture is worth a thousand words. Skype will add the country code for you. I sometimes use a two-digit variation of the 24-hour clock here. For numbers larger than 12, subtract 12 for p.m. times. Now don't get all worried; go have some fun! The Pacific is at your fingertips!

Key to Symbols: Here are some symbols, shorthand and abbreviations used here:

— $bed = lowest price for a dorm bed that we can find for a typical day, for comparison only (they change with seasons, promotions, and currency fluctuations)

— B'fast = Breakfast (free or not or for purchase only); don't expect much.

— c.c. = credit card, OK meaning they're accepted, +/% indicating a surcharge for use;

— Recep = times when there should be someone to check you in. Don't press your luck.

— 24/7 = they never close, supposedly. I suggest advising & confirming late arrival.

— HI, YHA, etc. are clubs that require a small fee; you'll gradually obtain membership.

— central = hostel is centrally located in the city, generally a good thing.

— cash only = even if you reserved with plastic, they want cash for the balance

— luggage room =you can stash your luggage to pick up later, very handy

— Y.H. = Youth Hostel

— lift = elevator, mate

— CBD = Central Business District = city center = 'downtown'

— *Jack1Free@ hypertravel.biz/* (for example) = my way of contracting e-mail addresses contained within domains. The second half is the website address (add 'www' if necessary). All listings contain websites; some have forms inside for contacting.

Note: on other related websites: you will also see a mini-UK flag on websites to indicate English language. That's the Union Jack, Jack.

Introduction to Australia, New Zealand, & Pacific Islands

The Pacific Ocean region is one of the least understood regions of the world, in something of an inverse proportion to its vastness. We're talking about a third of the planet's surface—mostly water—here, remember, with barely five percent of its population, so something of a statistical and geopolitical anomaly. There are some fifteen independent countries in the region, so that means all are equally represented here, right? No; in fact nothing could be more wrong. For not only does the Pacific Ocean region contain some of the most sparsely-populated countries in the world, with UN members Nauru and Tuvalu barely surpassing 10,000 inhabitants, but some of the most famous islands—say Easter Island, or Tahiti, for instance—owe allegiance to distant capitals in Chile and France, respectively, the latter of which generates much of the region's tourist income. Hawaii is treated separately in the book on North America.

Australia is the elephant in the room, of course, at one and the same time both country and continent, and containing much of the region's land area, while remaining outside the definition of what most people would consider "Pacific" or "oceanic," something more like overseas-Anglo culturally and politically. Factor in similarly Anglo little brother New Zealand, and what's left may seem like a vast empty water-world whose islands serve as little more than stepping stones between the Americas and Asia. Beyond the near-Asian population centers of Indonesia and the Philippines, that would be largely true. But that would be a vast over-simplification, of course. The Pacific region has a cultural richness far superior to its population numbers, and in its antiquity is second only to Africa, in fact. When fully modern *homo sapiens sapiens* finally got up off its collective ass and got the hell out of Africa, this is precisely where they came.

Australian aborigines, Phillippine 'negritos,' and Papuans are the descendants of those early migrations. By some estimates fully half of the world's ten or so modern races belong to the South Pacific region, the result of ancient migrations and multiple dead ends in the vast region, loosely represented by today's Austronesians—Malays, Indonesians, Filipinos, Polynesians, Melanesians, and Micronesians — in addition to the earlier groups already mentioned. And here they continue to exist to this day. The fact that these later groups apparently all hopped off the mainland at or around the island now known as Taiwan at a time barely beyond the purview of modern historians is another story, and beyond the scope of this summary. I'm sorry about that, Mr. Heyerdahl.

The vastness and the diversity of the region means that decisions must be made as to who and where gets included in this book, and where to draw the lines that separate Oceania and Asia. The original idea was to include them both together, by the way. I'll mostly forgo the use of the term "Oceania," though, as that gets too messy. There is another theory that the Austronesians were a Sunda peninsula phenomenon, but that apparently seems to apply only to those original kinky-haired aboriginals. The cultures themselves offer some surprises. Anyone who sees the whole region through the sun-drenched frond-waving skirt-shaking postcards of Hawaii and Tahiti might be surprised... even shocked. Polynesians in fact can be some bad-ass mothers, especially where they've been exposed to the gang culture of the US and elsewhere.

At the other extreme are the equally bad-ass Papuans of New Guinea, just barely out of the Stone Age and with some ten percent of the world's languages, the result of ancient migrations, late discovery by Europeans, relatively large population, and the extreme isolation of its diverse peoples within its mountainous interior. Until recently tribes faced off against each other with clubs and spears. The region's culture is at its best—IMHO— somewhere in between, maybe around Fiji or Tonga. The Anglo cultures of Australia and New Zealand are fairly predictable, though, of course, and the rest can ultimately be highly rewarding, although not necessarily for the reasons you expect. Travel with an open mind, a healthy wallet, and a little imagination, and you'll do fine. Just don't expect the cruise-ship culture of the Caribbean; outside the Oz-NZ-Fiji triangle, it's mostly not like that here. The distances are just too great.

Part I: Australia

Australia was first settled some 40,000 to 50,000 years ago by immigrants who worked their way across from Africa and who must have had some knowledge of navigation techniques in order to make the final leg of the journey. These people eventually dispersed and settled into some 250 linguistic groups before eventually being visited by Austronesian Asians in the early years of recorded history. They were later joined by Melanesians at the Torres Strait where Australia and New Guinea come close to each other, and which must have once been joined by a land bridge; kangaroos' close relatives there live in trees. Fast forward to a more recent past and Australia was sighted by the Dutch in the early 1600's before being colonized by the British in the late 1700's. The first colonists were prisoners sent into exile from Great Britain, and the rest is history.

The last convict ship arrived in 1848, and the Gold Rush was on a few years later, drawing off some of the same men who once rushed to California, only to find hard work and troubles. The plight of the aboriginals in Australia was something close to genocide, though, with children routinely removed from their homes, full rights only accorded recently, and standards of living that rate as third-world even today. Australia's six separate self-governing colonies formally joined in a federation in 1901, and Australia officially became a commonwealth and dominion of the British Empire in 1907. It fought on the side of Europe and the Allies in the World Wars and emerged as a modern developed nation in the aftermath. The official policy of "white Australia" was only finally abandoned in the 1970's, and Australia gradually has become a liberal and at least somewhat multicultural nation.

Today Australia is the world's sixth-largest country by land area, with the twelfth-largest economy and the fifth-highest per capita income. Yes, that means prices are high, after years of low prices and low exchange rates. Exports of commodities are the mainstay of the economy, and business is good, what with nearby China's emergence as factory for the world. Still most of the population lives within a narrow eastern coastal strip starting north in Brisbane and extending south around the bulge to Adelaide. But for that it's still mostly an empty continent. Imagine the mainland US with its strip of cities along the west coast and then nothing much else in the interior until you arrive on the opposite coast with its great metropolis of… Charlotte. Welcome to Oz. Geographically Australia can be divided into various regions roughly defined by the seven states and territories which comprise the country: Queensland, Victoria, New South Wales, South Australia, Tasmania, Western Australia, and the Northern Territory.

Hostels in general are good, though free WiFi is rare. Many of the backpackers here are on "work holiday." That's how they get the crops picked without allowing poor Indonesians and Papuans in. Hard-partying locals are frequently banished from many of the "real" backpackers' hostels. They typically name their coasts here after precious metals and gems. Yes, they take their beaches seriously, and nowhere else in the world—except maybe Brazil—does the phrase, "Life's a beach," carry so much meaning. And not unlike the USA, here there is also an Australian Dream: 'quarter acre home and garden' for every family. At times it feels like southern Californian suburban auto-culture, clinging to the beach rather than memories. Still the main cities are well-defined and nice, and so are the hostels. The language is English. The currency is the Australian dollar (AUD). The phone code is +61. Call me.

www.australia.com/

1) Australian Capital Territory

CANBERRRA is the purpose-built capital of Australia, with a population of some 367,000 at last count. It came into this world in 1908 as a result of competition between Sydney and Melbourne. An inland location, it has been inhabited seasonally since antiquity, by various indigenous groups, including the Ngunnawal people, the Ngarigo people, the Wandandian, the Walgulu, the Gandangara people, and Wiradjuri. There are rock paintings and engravings, burial places, camps and quarry sites, and stone tools to document continued habitation for more than 20,000 years. European exploration began in the 1800's.

The area was chosen to be capital in 1908; it was named in 1913; it opened for the business of Parliament in 1927. As a planned city and capital, government is the big engine of employment, and civic monuments the lion's share of landmarks. These include the Australian War Memorial, the National Gallery of Australia, the National Portrait Gallery, the National Library, the National Archives, the Australian Academy of Science, the National Film and Sound Archive, the National Museum, and many more. Festivals include the National Folk Festival, the Royal Canberra Show, the Summernats Car Festival, the Canberra Multicultural Festival, Celebrate Canberra, and Stonefest. There are many pubs and clubs. It's more expensive than most of Australia.

www.canberra.com.au/

Canberra YHA, 7 Akuna Street, Canberra, ACT; T:+61/262489155, *canberracity@ yha.com.au/*; $33bed, Kitchen:Y, B'fast:$, WiFi:Y, Pvt.room:Y,

1

Locker:Y, Recep:24/7; Note: billiards, tour desk, laundry, c.c. ok, wh/chair ok, pool, a/c, bike rent

Dickson B'packers, 4-14 Woolley St, Dickson ACT; *dicksonbackpackers. com.au/*, T:0262629922, *dicksonbackpackers@hotmail.com*; $34bed, Kitchen:Y, B'fast:N, WiFi:Y, Pvt.room:Y, Locker:Y, Recep:>10p; Note: Chinatown, parking, c.c. ok, laundry, billiards, a/c, bus>center

2) New South Wales, Australia

BLUE MOUNTAINS form a region due west of Sydney in New South Wales, its highest peak reaching some 1200m/4000ft above sea level, and its parks constituting a world heritage site. The original inhabitants were the Gundungurra—now based in Katoomba—and the Darug people. The area is popular for outdoor sports activities and features the "world's steepest railway."
www.bluemts.com.au/

No14, 14 Lovel St, Katoomba, NSW Blue Mountains; T:+61/247827104, *info@ no14.com.au*; $26bed, Kitchen:Y, B'fast:Y, WiFi:Y, Pvt.room:Y, Locker:N, Recep:ltd; Note: luggage room, laundry, c.c. ok, quiet

Blue Mountains YHA, 207 Katoomba St, Katoomba NSW; T:0247821416, *bluemountains@ yha.com.au*; $33bed, Kitchen:Y, B'fast:N, WiFi:Y, Pvt. room:Y, Locker:N, Recep:ltd; Note: billiards, tour desk, laundry, c.c. ok, wh/chair ok

The Flying Fox Backpackers, 190 Bathrurst Rd, Katoomba NSW; T:(02)47824226, *book@ theflyingfox.com.au/*; $30bed, Kitchen:Y, B'fast:Y, WiFi:Y, Pvt.room:Y, Locker:Y, Recep:ltd; Note: c.c. ok, bikes, luggage rm, laundry, CBD, near train, noon lockout

Katoomba Mountain Lodge, 31 Lurline St, Katoomba NSW; T:0247823933, *stay@ katoombamountainlodge.com.au/*; $24bed, Kitchen:Y, B'fast:N, WiFi:Y, Pvt. room:Y, Locker:N, Recep:ltd; Note: parking, c.c. ok, laundry, nice old house, central

BYRON BAY is a beach town a hundred miles south of Brisbane on the east coast of Australia, with a permanent population of around five thousand. Its first industry was cedar logging. Later came surfing. In 1973, when the Aquarius Festival was held in nearby Nimbin, its reputation as a hippy alternative town was established. Walking and cycling are encouraged. Besides surfing, whale-watching, scuba-diving and snorkeling are popular. There are frequent music and film festivals, yoga retreats and pagan gatherings. There are regular markets for crafts and produce. *Viva los 60!*
www.byronnaturally.com.au/

Cape Byron YHA, Middleton St, Byron Bay NSW; T:(02)66858788 *capebyron@ yha.com.au/*; $33bed, Kitchen:Y, B'fast:N, WiFi:Y, Pvt.room:Y, Locker:N, Recep:ltd; Note: billiards, tour desk, pool, c.c. ok, bikes, luggage room, c.c. ok

Byron Beach Resort, 25 Childe St, Byron Bay NSW; T:0266857868, *info@ byronbeachresort.com.au/*; $20bed, Kitchen:Y, B'fast:N, WiFi:Y, Pvt.room:Y, Locker:, Recep:ltd; Note: resto/bar, wh/chair ok, tour desk, safe dep, c.c. ok, bikes, parking

Nomads Byron Bay, 1 Lawson St, Byron Bay NSW, T:0266807966

Arts Factory Lodge, 1 Skinners Shoot Rd, Byron Bay, T:1800NOMADS, T:0266857709, *bookings@ nomadsworld.com*; $35bed, Kitchen:Y, B'fast:N, WiFi:$, Pvt.room:Y, Locker:Y, Recep:24/7; Note: parking, billiards, free tour/info, pool, c.c. ok, resto/bar, luggage $

COFFS HARBOUR lies on the east coast of Australia between Sydney and Brisbane. It currently has a population of 70,000 and counting. There is manufacturing, banana farming and tourism, but one of the big draws is its agreeable climate and its small-town atmosphere. The city is surrounded by national parks.

www.coffsharbour.nsw.gov.au

Aussitel Backpackers, 312 Harbour Dr, Coffs Harbour NSW; T:(02)66511871, *fun@ aussitel.com/*; $24bed, Kitchen:Y, B'fast:N, WiFi:Y, Pvt. room:Y, Locker:Y, Recep:ltd; Note: bikes, wh/chair ok, laundry, pool, billiards, luggage rm, arpt p-u

Plantation Backpackers, 88 Grafton St, Coffs Harbour NSW; T:(02)66523855, *plantationhotel.com.au/*; $26bed, Kitchen:Y, B'fast:N, WiFi:Y, Pvt.room:Y, Locker:Y, Recep:ltd; Note: beach shuttle, CBD, resto/bar, laundry, billiards, luggage rm

MERIMBULA is a city of 110,000 on the lake of the same name and situated almost equidistant between Sydney and Melbourne on the so-called "sapphire coast." It is predominantly a tourist town, with five beaches and three national parks in the vicinity.

www.merimbulatourism.com.au/

Wandarrah Lodge/Merimbula YHA, 8 Marine Parade, Merimbula; *yha. com.au/*, T:(02)64953503, *wanlodge@asitis.net.au*; $33bed, Kitchen:Y, B'fast:$, WiFi:Y, Pvt. room:Y, Locker:Y, Recep:ltd; Note: parking, wh/chair ok, laundry, arpt pickup, billiards, luggage rm $

NAROOMA is a small town of 3100 on the far south coast of New South Wales. Montague Island is 5mi/8km offshore. Besides that, Mount Gulaga and the historical gold rush town of Tilba Tilba are of tourist interest.

www.narooma.org.au/

Narooma Motel YHA, 243 Princes Highway, Narooma NSW; *narooma. org.au/*, T:(02)44763287, *naroomayha@iprimus.com.au*; $27bed, Kitchen:Y, B'fast:N, WiFi:Y, Pvt.room:Y, Locker:Y, Recep:ltd; Note: parking, c.c. ok, tour desk

2) New South Wales, Australia

NEWCASTLE is the second largest city of New South Wales, and is located some 100mi/160km north of the capital Sydney. Awabakal and Worimi Aboriginal People were here first. Since Europeans landed in 1797, it's been famous for its coal, something of little interest to most tourists, but of much interest to China. For tourists there are the Newcastle Regional Show, the Newcastle Jazz Festival, the Shoot Out 24 Hour Filmmaking Festival, and This Is Not Art, including Electrofringe, the National Young Writers' Festival, Critical Animals, Sound Summit, Crack Theatre Festival, and more.
www.visitnewcastle.com.au/

Blacksmiths Beach House, 6 Mitti St, Blacksmiths NSW; T:(02)49716901, *blacksmithsbeachhouse.com.au/*; $42bed, Kitchen:Y, B'fast:N, WiFi:Y, Pvt.room:Y, Locker:N, Recep:24/7; Note: parking, wh/chair ok, laundry, c.c. ok, near beach far from city

PORT MACQUARIE was founded as the original penal settlement for the baddest apples, its thick bush and rough terrain making it easy to hide out. Nowadays retirees are much of the 40,000 population, they and koalas in the Billabong Koala Park, and the Koala Preservation Society's Koala Hospital. I hope they've got guaranteed health coverage. There are flights to Sydney and Brisbane.
www.portmacquarieinfo.com.au/

Ozzie Pozzie B'packers/Port Macquarie YHA, 36 Waugh St, Port Macq NSW; T:0265838133, *portmacquarie@ yha.com.au*; $31bed, Kitchen:Y, B'fast:N, WiFi:Y, Pvt.room:Y, Locker:Y, Recep:>11p; Note: arpt p-u, bikes, wh/chair ok, pool, luggage rm, billiards, c.c. ok

PORT STEPHENS is a natural harbor 100mi/160km northeast of Sydney, larger than Sydney's harbor even, with major inflows from the Karuah and Myall Rivers. There are nature reserves at Cabbage Tree Island and Boondelbah Island, and a larger one at Port Stephens-Great Lakes Marine Park. In addition there are beaches, fishing, and retirement communities, almost 30,000 living within 2mi/3km of the shoreline.
www.portstephens.org.au/

Melaleuca Surfside B'packers, 2 Koala Pl, Boat Harbour NSW; *melaleucabackpackers@bigpond.com*; T:0249819422, *melaleucabackpackers.com.au/*; $33bed, Kitchen:Y, B'fast:N, WiFi:Y, Pvt.room:Y, Locker:N, Recep:ltd; Note: wh/chair ok, bikes, luggage rm, c.c. ok, tour desk, beach, forest

SYDNEY is Australia's largest city and capital of the state of New South Wales, with some four and a half million people calling it home, at last count. It is Australia's number one city by most measures, much to Melbourne's dismay. The traditional indigenous inhabitants of Sydney Cove are the Cadigal people, with tens of thousands of years of continuous habitation until James Cook showed up in 1770. They were soon decimated by smallpox and warfare, and the city of Sydney developed quickly, spurred by the gold rushes of the 1850's. Historic buildings of that period still standing include Sydney Town Hall, The Queen Victoria Building, Parliament House, and the Australian Museum. Sydney's most famous architectural monument, though, is a more modern one, the Sydney Opera House, now a world heritage site.

The hub of most aspects of Australian life, Sydney is also the hub of culture, with such institutions as the Art Gallery of New South Wales, the Museum of Contemporary Art, the Museum of Sydney and the Powerhouse Museum. Besides the Sydney Festival — Australia's largest — festivals include the Biennale of Sydney, the Big Day Out, Sculpture by the Sea, the Gay and Lesbian Mardi Gras, the Sydney Film Festival, and the smaller Tropfest and Flickerfest. And besides the renowned Opera House, for theatre there are the Sydney Town Hall, City Recital Hall, the State Theatre, the Theatre Royal Sydney, the Sydney Theatre, the Wharf Theatre, and the Capitol Theatre.

Sydney is one of the world's great cities, and long ago splintered into suburbs and neighborhoods great in their own right, such as Parramatta in the central-west, Penrith in the west, Bondi Junction in the east, Liverpool southwest, Chatswood to the north, and Hurstville to the south. Sydney receives almost three million visitors every year, and more than a few of them backpackers. In addition to everything else, Sydney is one of the great hostel cities of the world, and one of the few where you could disembark at grand central station, start walking, and likely find one. I'd still advise calling ahead though, or book in advance. The list below is fairly comprehensive.

www.sydney.com/

2) New South Wales, Australia

City Resort Hostel, 103-105 Palmer St, Woolloomooloo NSW; T:(02)93573333, *info@ cityresort.com.au/*; $31bed, Kitchen:Y, B'fast:N, WiFi:Y, Pvt.room:Y, Locker:N, Recep:ltd; Note: tour info, laundry, c.c. ok, safe deposit, party, basic

Sydney Central YHA, 11 Rawson Pl, (Cnr Pitt), Sydney NSW; T:+61/292189000, *sydcentral@ yha.com.au/*; $38bed, Kitchen:Y, B'fast:$, WiFi:Y, Pvt.room:Y, Locker:Y, Recep:24/7; Note: pool, billiards, wh/chair ok, resto/bar, tour desk, laundry, near train

Maze Backpackers, 417 Pitt St, Sydney NSW; T:0292115115, *info@ mazebackpackers.com/*; $24bed, Kitchen:Y, B'fast:N, WiFi:Y, Pvt.room:Y, Locker:N, Recep:24/7; Note: party, meals, arpt pickup, free tour/info, laundry, luggage rm, central

Nomads Westend Backpackers, 412 Pitt St, Sydney NSW; T:(02)92114588, *bookings@ nomadsworld.com/*; $27bed, Kitchen:Y, B'fast:N, WiFi:$, Pvt.room:Y, Locker:Y, Recep:24/7; Note: food, wh/chair ok, lift, free tour/info, laundry, luggage $, lift, CBD

Bounce Hotel, 28 Chalmers St, Sydney NSW; T:(02)92812222, *info@ bouncehotel.com.au/*; $36bed, Kitchen:Y, B'fast:N, WiFi:Y, Pvt.room:Y, Locker:Y, Recep:24/7; Note: resto/bar, wh/chair ok, lift, free tour/info, laundry, luggage $, c.c. ok

Sydney Harbour YHA, 110 Cumberland St, Sydney NSW; T:+(612)82720950, *sydneyharbour@ yha.com.au/*; $42bed, Kitchen:Y, B'fast:N, WiFi:Y, Pvt.room:Y, Locker:$, Recep:24/7; Note: wh/chair ok, tour desk, laundry, a/c, c.c. ok, central, pub tour, roof

World Square Hostel, 2/640 George St, Sydney NSW; T:(02)92675616, *info@ worldsquarehostel.com.au/*; $29bed, Kitchen:Y, B'fast:N, WiFi:Y, Pvt.room:Y, Locker:Y, Recep:24/7; Note: bar/club, luggage room, tour desk, laundry, a/c, c.c. ok, lift

Base Sydney, 477 Kent St, Sydney NSW; T:+61/292677718, *sydney@ stayatbase.com/*; $32bed, Kitchen:Y, B'fast:$, WiFi:Y, Pvt.room:Y, Locker:Y,

Recep:24/7; Note: wh/chair ok, tour desk, laundry, a/c, c.c. ok, billiards, club, central

Wake Up Hostel, 509 Pitt St, Sydney NSW; *wakeup.com.au/*, T:+61/292887888; $35bed, Kitchen:Y, B'fast:$, WiFi:$, Pvt.room:Y, Locker:Y, Recep:24/7; Note: resto/bar, a/c, c.c. ok, lift, free tour/info, laundry, central

Glebe Point YHA, 262-264 Glebe Point Road, Sydney; T:+61/296928418, *glebe@ yha.com.au/*; $31bed, Kitchen:Y, B'fast:Y, WiFi:Y, Pvt.room:Y, Locker:Y, Recep:8a>8p; Note: village vibe, non-CBD, luggage rm, tour desk, laundry, a/c, c.c. ok

Sydney Beachouse YHA, 4 Collaroy St, NSW; T:(02)99811177, *collaroy@ yha.com.au/*; $35bed, Kitchen:Y, B'fast:N, WiFi:Y, Pvt.room:Y, Locker:Y, Recep:ltd; Note: pool, billiards, wh/chair ok, tour desk, laundry, a/c, c.c. ok, far

Cambridge Lodge, 109 Cambridge St, Stanmore NSW; T:(02)95646822, *cambridgelodge.com.au/*; $31bed, Kitchen:Y, B'fast:Y, WiFi:Y, Pvt.room:Y, Locker:N, Recep:8a>8p; Note: non-CBD, luggage rm, tour desk, laundry, parking, c.c.ok

Y Hotel Hyde Park, 5-11 Wentworth Ave, Sydney NSW; *yhotel.com.au/*, T:(02)92642451, *enquiry@yhotels.com*; $53bed, Kitchen:Y, B'fast:Y, WiFi:Y, Pvt.room:Y, Locker:Y, Recep:24/7; Note: wh/chair ok, tour desk, laundry, a/c, c.c. ok, safe dep, luggage rm

BIG Hostel, 212 Elizabeth St, Sydney NSW; *bighostel.com/*, T:(02)92816030; $31bed, Kitchen:Y, B'fast:Y, WiFi:Y, Pvt.room:Y, Locker:Y, Recep:24/7; Note: wh/chair ok, tour desk, laundry, a/c, c.c. ok, luggage rm, roof terrace

Kings Cross Backpackers, 79 Bayswater Rd, Sydney; T:(02)93310520, *info@ kingscrossbackpackers.com.au/*; $38bed, Kitchen:Y, B'fast:Y, WiFi:Y, Pvt.room:N, Locker:Y, Recep:>12m; Note: arpt pickup, free tour/info, laundry, a/c, c.c. ok, luggage rm, nightlife

Casa Central Accommodation, 11 Regent St, Chippendale NSW; *casacentral. com.au/* ; T:0404246003, *casaradiante1@hotmail.com*; $31bed, Kitchen:Y, B'fast:N, WiFi:Y, Pvt.room:Y, Locker:Y, Recep:>10p; Note: laundry, c.c. ok, central, quiet

Jolly Swagman Backpackers, 27 Orwell St, Potts Point NSW; T:(02)93586400, *stay@ jollyswagman.com.au/*; $35bed, Kitchen:Y, B'fast:Y, WiFi:Y, Pvt.room:Y, Locker:Y, Recep:24/7; Note: arpt pickup, party, laundry, c.c. ok, central, games

Elephant B'packer Sydney, 50 Sir John Young Crescent, Woollomoloo; *elephantbackpacker.com.au/*, T:1800882922, $25bed, Kitchen:Y, B'fast:N, *harborcityhotel@bigpond.com;* WiFi:Y, Pvt.room:Y, Locker:Y, Recep:24/7; Note: resto/bar, wh/chair ok, lift, tour desk, laundry, pool, activities

Alfred Park Accommodation, 207 Cleveland St, Redfern NSW; T:(02)93194031, *bookings@ alfredpark.com.au/*; $25bed, Kitchen:Y, B'fast:N, WiFi:Y, Pvt.room:Y, Locker:Y, Recep:ltd; Note: luggage rm, tour desk, laundry, parking, c.c.ok, a/c, arpt pickup

City Central Budget Accommodation, 707 George St, Sydney NSW; T:(02)92119999, *budget@ ccbackpack.com.au/*; $29bed, Kitchen:Y, B'fast:N, WiFi:Y, Pvt.room:N, Locker:Y, Recep:ltd; Note: luggage rm, tour desk, laundry, safe deposit, TV, Chinatown

Mountbatten Hotel, 701 George St, Sydney NSW; T:01752484660, *info@ hotelmountbatten.co.uk/*; $23bed, Kitchen:Y, B'fast:Y, WiFi:Y, Pvt.room:Y, Locker:Y, Recep:ltd; Note: resto/bar, tour desk, laundry, TV, c.c. ok

Sydney Backpackers, 7 Wilmot St, Sydney NSW; T:0292677772, *info@ sydneybackpackers.com/*; $27bed, Kitchen:Y, B'fast:N, WiFi:Y, Pvt.room:N, Locker:Y, Recep:>11p; Note: wh/chair ok, tour desk, laundry, a/c, c.c. ok, luggage room, central

Brado's Backpackers, 34-36 Darlinghurst Rd, Potts Point NSW; *bradosbackpackers.com/*, TF:1800768505, T:+61/293585505; $25bed, Kitchen:Y, B'fast:Y, WiFi:Y, Pvt.room:Y, Locker:Y, Recep:8a>9p; Note: no locals, arpt pickup $, free tour/info, a/c, c.c. ok, luggage room

Sydney Central B'packers, 16 Orwell St, Potts Point; T:(02)93586600, *info@ sydneybackpackers.com.au/*; $30bed, Kitchen:N, B'fast:Y, WiFi:Y, Pvt.room:Y, Locker:N, Recep:ltd; Note: tour desk, laundry, c.c. ok, luggage room, free arpt pickup

Boomerang Backpackers, 141 William St, Sydney NSW; T:0283540488, *info@ boomerangbackpackers.com/*; $20bed, Kitchen:Y, B'fast:Y, WiFi:Y, Pvt. room:N, Locker:Y, Recep:ltd; Note: no locals, arpt pickup $, free tour/info, laundry, c.c. ok

Central Perk Backpackers, 611 George St, Sydney NSW; T:0292112604, *reception@ cpbackpackers.com.au/*; $29bed, Kitchen:Y, B'fast:Y, WiFi:Y, Pvt. room:N, Locker:Y, Recep:ltd; Note: tour desk, laundry, c.c. ok, luggage room

Glebe Village Backpackers, 256 Glebe Point Rd, Glebe NSW; T:(02)96608133, *info@ glebevillage.com/*; $23bed, Kitchen:Y, B'fast:N, WiFi:Y, Pvt.room:Y, Locker:N, Recep:ltd; Note: tour desk, laundry, c.c. ok, luggage room, safe deposit, far, no lift

Sydney G'Day Backpackers, 153 Forbes St, Woolloomooloo NSW; *g-day. com.au/*, T:(02)93584327; $29bed, Kitchen:Y, B'fast:N, WiFi:Y, Pvt.room:N, Locker:Y, Recep:8a>10p; Note: no locals, arpt pickup $, free tour/info, laundry, c.c. ok

Tokyo Village, 243-247 Cleveland St, Redfern NSW; T:(02)96988839, *info@ tokyovillage.com.au/*; $25bed, Kitchen:Y, B'fast:N, WiFi:Y, Pvt.room:Y, Locker:Y, Recep:ltd; Note: laundry, c.c. ok, luggage room, safe deposit, family atmosphere

Home Backpackers, 238 Elizabeth St, Sydney NSW; T:0292119111, *info@ homebackpackers.com/*; $22bed, Kitchen:Y, B'fast:N, WiFi:Y, Pvt.room:Y, Locker:Y, Recep:8a-8p; Note: tour desk, c.c. ok, central

Manly Backpackers, 24-28 Raglan St, Manly NSW; T:0299773411, *info@ manlybackpackers.com.au/*; $27bed, Kitchen:N, B'fast:N, WiFi:Y, Pvt.room:Y, Locker:N, Recep:ltd; Note: luggage rm, billiards, c.c. ok, parking, laundry, party, beach

2) New South Wales, Australia

Boardrider Backpacker/Budget Motel, 63 The Corso, Manly NSW; T:(02)99776077, *info@ boardrider.com.au/*; $24bed, Kitchen:Y, B'fast:N, WiFi:Y, Pvt. room:Y, Locker:Y, Recep:ltd; Note: lift, wh/chair ok, tour desk, laundry, c.c. ok, surf

Kanga House, 141 Victoria St, NSW, Australia; T:(02)93577897, *info@ kangahouse.com.au/*; $27bed, Kitchen:Y, B'fast:Y, WiFi:Y, Pvt.room:Y, Locker:Y, Recep:ltd; Note: laundry, c.c. ok, luggage room, free arpt pickup

Australian Backpackers, 132 Bourke St, Woolloomooloo NSW; 0293316684, *info@ australianbackpackers.net/*; $24bed, Kitchen:Y, B'fast:Y, WiFi:Y, Pvt. room:N, Locker:N, Recep:ltd; Note: rooftop, cheap/basic

SYDNEY/BONDI BEACH is 4mi/7km east of the CBD. Formerly a working-class suburb, it is in the process of gentrification, though still diverse. It was previously the scene of swimsuit decency campaigns. There are rip currents, no pun intended.
   www.sydney.com.au/bondi-beach.htm

Bondi Shores, 1/283 Bondi Rd, Bondi NSW; *bondishores.com.au/*, T:1800330010, *bondishores@gmail.com*; $29bed, Kitchen:Y, B'fast:Y, WiFi:Y, Pvt. room:Y, Locker:Y, Recep:>9p; Note: resto/bar, luggage $, billiards, c.c. ok, free tour/info, laundry

Surfside Backpackers Bondi Beach, 35A Hall St, Bondi NSW; T:0293654900, *bondi@ surfsidebackpackers.com.au/*; $24bed, Kitchen:Y, B'fast:N, WiFi:Y, Pvt.room:Y, Locker:Y, Recep:ltd; Note: tour desk, laundry, safe deposit, c.c. ok, beach

Lamrock Lodge on Bondi Beach, 19 Lamrock Ave, Bondi Beach NSW; *lamrocklodge.com/*, T:(02)91305063; $27bed, Kitchen:Y, B'fast:N, WiFi:Y, Pvt. room:Y, Locker:N, Recep:ltd; Note: tour desk, laundry, safe deposit, c.c. ok, luggage rm, lift

SYDNEY/COOGEE BEACH is a suburb 5mi/8km southeast of the CBD, popular for swimming.
   coogeebeach.net.au/

11

Surfside B'packers Coogee Beach, 186 Arden St, Coogee Bch-over McD; T:0293157888, *coogee@ surfsidebackpackers.com.au/*; $36bed, Kitchen:Y, B'fast:N, WiFi:Y, Pvt.room:Y, Locker:N, Recep:ltd; Note: resto/bar, luggage rm, c.c. ok, tour info, laundry, safe deposit

Coogee Beach House, 171 Arden St, Coogee NSW; T:0296651162, *info@ coogeebeachhouse.com/*; $26bed, Kitchen:Y, B'fast:Y, WiFi:Y, Pvt.room:Y, Locker:Y, Recep:ltd; Note: forex, c.c. ok, tour desk, luggage room, beach

3) Northern Territories, Australia

ALICE SPRINGS sits smack in the center of Australia, in the vast open red sand desert that once defined the pre-European pre-surf country. It was once a stronghold of Aboriginal groups, of which the Aranda, or Arrernte, were — and still are — the most important. Other important groups within the almost 30,000 population include American soldiers as part of the joint military Detachment 421 and... the highest percentage of lesbians in the country. Keep your hands to yourself. It is known as "Aboriginal Art Capital of Central Australia" and the annual Desert Mob Art Show brings in buyers and collectors from all over the world. It sits on the main non-coastal north-south highway with regular bus and air connections.

www.tourism.thealice.com.au/

Annie's Place Hostel, 4 Traeger Ave, Alice Springs NT; T:1800818011, *info@ anniesplace.com.au/*; $21bed, Kitchen:Y, B'fast:Y, WiFi:Y, Pvt.room:Y, Locker:N, Recep:ltd; Note: central, arpt pickup, pool, c.c. ok, resto/bar, tour desk, bikes

Alice Lodge Backpackers, 4 Mueller St, Alice Springs NT; T:(08)89531975, *info@ alicelodge.com.au/*; $22bed, Kitchen:Y, B'fast:Y, WiFi:Y, Pvt.room:Y,

Locker:Y, Recep:ltd; Note: central, arpt pickup, pool, c.c. ok, tour desk, laundry, parking

Toddys Backpackers, 41 Gap Road, The Gap NT; T:(08)8952 1322, *toddys@ toddys.com.au/*; $24bed, Kitchen:Y, B'fast:Y, WiFi:Y, Pvt.room:Y, Locker:N, Recep:ltd; Note: wh/chair ok, arpt pickup, pool, far, resto/bar, luggage rm, tour desk

DARWIN is the capital and largest city of the Northern Territory, with more than 125,000 inhabitants. Once a remote northern outpost and home of the Larrakia people, it is now a budding multicultural city and the only city of any importance for hundreds of miles in any direction. Its tropical location keeps it warm to hot year-round, the wet and the dry being the two seasons. It is named for the legendary biologist, who visited the area in 1836. But he was not the first. The Dutch had mapped the coast for a couple centuries from their bases in Indonesia, and Indonesians from Makassar had carried on a trade in sea cucumbers for almost as long. The Larrakia themselves had land routes based on 'songlines' with the remotest corners of Australia. Thus a primitive trade route had long been established.

There was a gold rush in the early 1870's. Trade union unrest culminated in the Darwin Rebellion in December 1918. Darwin was attacked by the Japanese in 1942, largely destroying the town. It was totally destroyed by Cyclone Tracy in 1974. The Darwin-Adelaide Railway was completed in 2003. Energy production and mining dominate the economy, but tourism is the new gold rush, thanks to kilometers of unspoilt beaches and constant festivals and markets. Best-known among these are the Mindil Beach Sunset Markets, the Parap Market, Nightcliff Market and Rapid Creek market; and the annual Darwin Festival, the NT Indigenous Music Awards, the Glenti Greek festival, India@Mindil, and Chinese New Year. Alternative lifestyles are engrained in Darwin culture, and aboriginal culture is appreciated.

www.travelnt.com/

Youth Shack Hostel, 69 Mitchell St, Darwin NT; T:1300793302, *info@ youthshack.com.au/*; $29bed, Kitchen:Y, B'fast:N, WiFi:Y, Pvt.room:Y, Locker:Y, Recep:ltd; Note: center, billiards, arpt pickup, pool, c.c. ok, bar, luggage rm, tour desk

Chilli's Backpackers Hostel, 69 Mitchell St, Darwin NT; T:1800351313, *info@ chillis.com.au/*; $29bed, Kitchen:Y, B'fast:Y, WiFi:Y, Pvt.room:Y, Locker:Y, Recep:ltd; Note: tour desk, c.c. ok, a/c, luggage room, laundry, safe deposit, central

Melaleuca on Mitchell Backpacker, 52 Mitchell St, Darwin NT; T:(08)89417800, *info@ momdarwin.com/*; $30bed, Kitchen:Y, B'fast:N, Wi-Fi:Y, Pvt.room:Y, Locker:Y, Recep:24/7; Note: billiards, tour desk, laundry, c.c. ok, bar, wh/chair ok, bar, pool, a/c

Banyan View Lodge, 119 Mitchell St, Darwin NT; T:(08)89818644, *banyanviewlodge.com.au/,;* $30bed, Kitchen:Y, B'fast:$, WiFi:Y, Pvt.room:Y, Locker:Y, Recep:ltd; Note: parking, tour info, pool, a/c, safe deposit, luggage $, c.c. ok

Darwin YHA, 97 Mitchell St, Darwin NT; T:(08)89815385, *darwin@ yha. com.au/*; $33bed, Kitchen:Y, B'fast:N, WiFi:Y, Pvt.room:Y, Locker:N, Recep:ltd; Note: luggage room, tour desk, laundry, c.c. ok, bar, pool, a/c, center

KATHERINE is a town of almost 6000 people, located 200mi/320km southeast of Darwin. It is the closest town to RA Air Force base Tindal, and is a transportation hub and mining center. It is also gateway to Nitmiluk National Park, including Katherine Gorge and the ancient rock paintings of the Jawoyn and Wardaman people. Agriculture is important, too.
   www.travelnt.com/katherine-and-surrounds.aspx

Palm Court Backpackers, Giles St. & Third St, Katherine, NT; *palmcourtbackpackers.com/*, 1800626722, *palmcourt1@bigpond.com.au*; $28bed, Kitchen:Y, B'fast:N, WiFi:Y, Pvt.room:Y, Locker:Y, Recep:ltd; Note: parking, laundry, pool, luggage rm, c.c. ok, near Nitmiluk natl park

TENNANT CREEK is a town of three thousand — one-third of them aboriginal — in the Northern Territtory, and is known mainly for its cattle stations. It has also been a center of gold mining. Cultural activities revolve around the Nyinkka Nyunyu Cultural Centre for Aboriginal people and the Winanjjikari Music Centre.

www.travelnt.com/tennant-creek-and-barkly-region.aspx

Tourist Rest VIP Tennant Creek YH, Leichhardt St, Tennant Creek NT; T:0889622719, *info@ touristrest.com.au/*; $27bed, Kitchen:Y, B'fast:Y, WiFi:Y, Pvt.room:Y, Locker:N, Recep:24/7; Note: arpt p-u, tour desk, pool, luggage rm, c.c. ok, parking

4) Queensland, Australia

AGNES WATER and Town of 1770 are somewhat interchangeable terms for that point along Australia's northern "Discovery Coast" where James Cook first came ashore way back when; I can't remember the year. For tourist purposes it's perhaps more important as the point where the southern surf beaches die out and the Great Barrier Reef takes over. You can't have both in the same place.

www.townof1770-agneswater.com.au

1770 Cool Bananas, 2 Springs Rd, Agnes Water, Australia QLD; *coolbananas.net.au/*, TF:1800227600, *wheeler_danny@hotmail.com*; $27bed, Kitchen:N, B'fast:N, WiFi:N, Pvt.room:Y, Locker:N, Recep:ltd; Note: free tour/info, laundry, c.c. ok, parking, wh/chair ok, bar, luggage rm

Beachside Backpacker, 12 Captain Cook Drive, Agnes Water, QLD; *facebook.com/pages/1770-Beachside-Backpacker/*, T:0749747200; $26beds, Kitchen:Y, B'fast:Y, WiFi:Y, Pvt.room:Y, Locker:Y, Recep:ltd; Note: billiards, tour desk, laundry, c.c. ok, bikes, wh/chair ok, pool, a/c

1770 Southern Cross Backpackers, 2694 Round Hill Rd, Agnes Water, QLD; TF:1800174225, *info@ 1770southerncross.com/*; $28bed, Kitchen:Y, B'fast:Y,

WiFi:Y, Pvt.room:Y, Locker:N, Recep:24/7; Note: billiards, tour desk, bar, c.c. ok, pool, a/c, luggage rm $, Bali style

1770 Backpackers, 22 Grahame Colyer Dr, Agnes Water QLD; *the1770backpackers.com.au/*, TF:1800121770; $23bed, Kitchen:Y, B'fast:N, WiFi:Y, Pvt.room:Y, Locker:N, Recep:24/7; Note: tour desk, parking, c.c. ok, central, wh/chair ok, surf, luggage rm $

AIRLIE BEACH is one of the more popular spots on the northern coast and a good jumping-off point for the Great Barrier Reef. It is far north enough to have a tropical climate (southern hemisphere, remember), and is well-known for the stinging jellyfish which inhabit its shores from November to May. Be careful.
www.airliebeach.com/

Base Airlie Beach Resort, 336 Shute Harbour Rd, Airlie Beach QLD; T:+61/749482000, *airliebeach@stayatbase.com/*; $23bed, Kitchen:Y, B'fast:N, WiFi:Y, Pvt.room:Y, Locker:N, Recep:ltd; Note: resto/bar, billiards, tour desk, pool, c.c. ok, luggage $

Airlie Waterfront Backpackers, 6 The Esplanade, Airlie Beach QLD; *airliewaterfront.com/*, T:+61749481300; $26bed, Kitchen:Y, B'fast:N, WiFi:Y, Pvt.room:Y, Locker:Y, Recep:7a>8p; Note: resto/bar, bikes, tour desk, c.c. ok, luggage $, a/c, free WiFi

Airlie Beach YHA, 394 Shute Harbour Rd, Airlie Beach QLD; T:(07)49466312, *airliebeach@ yha.com.au/*; $27bed, Kitchen:Y, B'fast:N, WiFi:Y, Pvt.room:Y, Locker:N, Recep:7a>7p; Note: tour desk, pool, c.c. ok, laundry, parking, central

Backpackers by the Bay, 12 Hermitage Dr, Airlie Beach QLD; TF:1800646994, *info@ backpackersbythebay.com/*; $28bed, Kitchen:Y, B'fast:N, WiFi:Y, Pvt.room:Y, Locker:N, Recep:ltd; Note: resto/bar, billiards, tour desk, pool, c.c. ok

Airlie Beach Magnums, 366 Shute Harbour Rd, Airlie Beach QLD; *magnums.com.au/*, T:(07)49641199; $20bed, Kitchen:N, B'fast:N, WiFi:Y, Pvt.

room:N, Locker:N, Recep:ltd; Note: resto/bar, wh/chair ok, tour desk, safe dep, c.c. ok, a/c, central

Bush Village Budget Cabins, 2 St Martins Rd, Whitsundays QLD; T:(07)49466177, *info@ bushvillage.com.au/*; $33bed, Kitchen:Y, B'fast:Y, WiFi:Y, Pvt.room:Y, Locker:N, Recep:ltd; Note: bar, parking, tour desk, pool, c.c. ok, a/c

ATHERTON TABLELANDS is the elevated area immediately west and south of Cairns in tropical Queensland, with fertile volcanic soils and mild climate. Originally it was a region for tin mining and timber, and sported one of the country's first Chinatowns, which pre-dated the town of Atherton. They in turn established agriculture and dairy farming in the region. Today Tinnaroo Lake and Dam is a tourist attraction.
www.athertontablelands.com.au/

On the Wallaby Backpackers Lodge, 34 Eacham Rd, Yungaburra QLD; T:(07)40952031, *info@ onthewallaby.com/*; $25bed, Kitchen:Y, B'fast:$, WiFi:Y, Pvt.room:Y, Locker:N, Recep:ltd; Note: parking, billiards, tour desk, c.c. ok, laundry, Cairns shuttle $

BRISBANE has over two million people, making it the northeastern state of Queensland's largest—and Australia's third-largest—city. A penal colony was first founded here in 1824 and free settlers were allowed from 1842. Prior to that, Brisbane was inhabited by the Turrbal and Jagera people. General McArthur was stationed here in WWII and over a million US soldiers passed through. It wasn't without problems. During the so-called "Battle of Brisbane" one person was killed and several were injured when Yanks and Aussies clashed. The 1974 Brisbane flood was a major disaster. World Expo 88 was a major success. Another major flood hit in January 2011 about a week after I left and while I was still in Fiji. I helped fellow Aussies look for their houses in the flood water on TV. Before that they had been plagued by droughts for a decade.

Brisbane has a Chinatown and Queen Street rules for retail. The cultural scene is lively, both art and music, led by the Queensland Performing Arts

Centre (QPAC) and the Queensland Gallery of Modern Art (GOMA), along with its neighbors the State Library of Queensland and the Queensland Art Gallery. There are several theaters, oldest among them the Brisbane Arts Theatre, and countless pubs and clubs. There are festivals of film, music, and food. Parks and sanctuaries are popular tourist destinations, including the South Bank Parklands, Roma Street Parkland, the City Botanic Gardens, Brisbane Forest Park, Portside Wharf, and the Lone Pine Koala Sanctuary. Sounds fun. It is.
www.visitbrisbane.com.au

Brisbane City YHA, 392 Upper Roma St, Brisbane QLD; T:+61/732361004, *brisbanecity@ yha.com.au/*; $34bed, Kitchen:Y, B'fast:N, WiFi:$, Pvt.room:Y, Locker:Y, Recep:24/7; Note: resto/bar, billiards, tour desk, pool, c.c, wh/chair ok, a/c, luggage rm

Bunk Backpackers, 11 Gipps St, Fortitude Valley QLD; *katarzyna.com.au/*, T:(07)3257 3644; $22bed, Kitchen:Y, B'fast:N, WiFi:$, Pvt.room:Y, Locker:$, Recep:24/7; Note: free meal, spa, resto/bar, billiards, pool, c.c. ok, wh/chair ok, a/c

Base Brisbane Ctr, 308 Edward St; T:0732112433, *brisbane@ stayatbase.com/*;

Base Brisbane-Embassy, 214 Elizabeth St, Brisbane City QLD; T:0731668000, *embassy@ stayatbase.com/*; $31bed, Kitchen:Y, B'fast:$, WiFi:$, Pvt.room:Y, Locker:Y, Recep:ltd; Note: bar, tour desk, laundry, c.c. ok, TV, luggage room, a/c, central

Brisbane Backpackers Resort, 110 Vulture St, West End QLD; T:0738449956; *info@ brisbanebackpackers.com.au/*; $28bed, Kitchen:Y, B'fast:Y, WiFi:$, Pvt.room:Y, Locker:N, Recep:24/7; Note: resto/bar, billiards, pool, c.c. ok, wh/chair ok, a/c, luggage rm

Somewhere To Stay, Cnr Brighton Rd/Franklin St, (West End), QLD; T:0738462858, *reception@ somewheretostay.com.au/*; $20bed, Kitchen:Y, B'fast:N, WiFi:Y, Pvt.room:Y, Locker:Y, Recep:24/7; Note: tour desk, pool, c.c. ok, wh/chair ok, a/c, luggage rm, laundry

Aussie Way Hostel, 34 Cricket St, Brisbane QLD; *aussiewaybackpackers.com/*, T:0733690711, *aussieway15@hotmail.com*; $27bed, Kitchen:Y, B'fast:N,

WiFi:Y, Pvt.room:Y, Locker:Y, Recep:ltd; Note: billiards, tour desk, pool, c.c. ok, laundry, a/c, luggage room

Tinbilly Travellers, 466 George Street, Brisbane QLD;, T:(07)32385888, *reservations@ tinbilly.com/*; $23bed, Kitchen:Y, B'fast:N, WiFi:Y, Pvt.room:Y, Locker:Y, Recep:24/7; Note: resto/bar, billiards, laundry, a/c, c.c. ok, safe deposit, central

Banana Bender Backpackers, 118 Petrie Terrace, Brisbane QLD; *bananabenders.com/*, T:(07)33671157; $27bed, Kitchen:Y, B'fast:N, WiFi:Y, Pvt. room:Y, Locker:N, Recep:ltd; Note: billiards, TV, c.c. ok, laundry, bar, luggage room, central

Valley Verandas Friendly Backpackers, 11 Grenier St, Spring Hill, QLD; *valleyverandas.com.au/*, TF:1800680320, T:0732521820; $25bed, Kitchen:Y, B'fast:N, WiFi:Y, Pvt.room:Y, Locker:Y, Recep:ltd; Note: pickups, laundry, c.c. ok, luggage room, not central

Prince Consort Backpackers, 230 Wickham St, Fortitude Valley QLD; T:(07)32572252, *info@ princeconsort.com.au/*; $27bed, Kitchen:Y, B'fast:N, WiFi:Y, Pvt.room:N, Locker:N, Recep:ltd; Note: cheap eats, resto/bar, billiards, laundry, a/c, c.c. ok, long-stays

Bowen Terrace Accommodation, 365 Bowen Terrace, New Farm QLD; *bowenterrace.com.au/*, T:(07)32540458; $35bed, Kitchen:Y, B'fast:N, WiFi:Y, Pvt. room:Y, Locker:N, Recep:ltd; Note: free WiFi, quiet, billiards, tour desk, pool, c.c. ok, laundry, parking

Bluetongue Backpackers & Tours, 515 Brunswick St, New Farm QLD; *bluetonguebackpackers.com.au/*, T:(07)32541984; $23bed, Kitchen:Y, B'fast:N, WiFi:Y, Pvt.room:Y, Locker:N, Recep:>8p; Note: no locals, laundry, c.c. ok, luggage room, not central, parking

Manly Harbour Backpackers, 1st/45 Cambridge Parade, Manly QLD; *manlyharbourbackpackers.com.au/*, T:(07)33963824; $26bed, Kitchen:Y, B'fast:Y, WiFi:Y, Pvt.room:Y, Locker:Y, Recep:ltd; Note: resto/bar, billiards, laundry, safe deposit, c.c. ok, not central

Cloud9 Backpackers, 350 Upper Roma St, Brisbane QLD; *cloud9backpackers. com.au/,* T:(07)32362333; $18bed, Kitchen:Y, B'fast:N, WiFi:Y, Pvt.room:Y, Locker:Y, Recep:Y; Note: bar, tour desk, a/c, c.c. ok, wh/chair ok, safe dep, central, basic

Yellow Submarine Backpackers, 66 Quay St, Brisbane QLD; *yellowsubmarinebackpackers.com/,* T:(07)32113424; $23bed, Kitchen:Y, B'fast:N, WiFi:Y, Pvt.room:Y, Locker:N, Recep:ltd; Note: billiards, free tour, pool, c.c., laundry, a/c, luggage rm, long-stays

Brisbane Manor Hotel, 555 Gregory Terrace, Fortitude Valley QLD; TF:1800800589, *reservations@ brisbanemanor.com/*; $26beds, Kitchen:Y, B'fast:N, WiFi:Y, Pvt.room:Y, Locker:N, Recep:ltd; Note: resto/bar, tour desk, laundry, safe deposit, c.c. ok, far>mkt, quiet

CAIRNS is a city of 150,000 on the east coast in the tropical zone of far north Queensland. Previously inhabited by the Walubarra Yidinji people, it was founded by Europeans in 1876 to serve gold miners, before becoming a railhead and transport hub for the region. The main tourist attraction is the Great Barrier Reef, which lies offshore and is one of the great natural phenomena of the world. Considering Cairns' small size and the fact that it does not even rate in the top ten for domestic tourism, it's interesting to note that it has a number of hostels second only to Sydney. That must mean something. Aboriginal culture is strong here.

www.cairns.com.au

Dreamtime Hostel, Cnr. Bunda & Terminus St., Cairns; T:0740316753, *info@ dreamtimehostel.com/*; $25bed, Kitchen:Y, B'fast:N, WiFi:Y, Pvt.room:Y, Locker:N, Recep:ltd; Note: pool, tour desk, laundry, c.c. ok, parking, luggage room, a/c

Nomads Esplanade, 89/93 Esplanade, Cairns QLD; 0740410378, *info@ nomadsesplanade.com.au/*; $25bed, Kitchen:Y, B'fast:Y, WiFi:Y, Pvt.room:Y, Locker:N, Recep:ltd; Note: arpt pickup, pool, laundry, c.c. ok, luggage room, a/c, lagoon

Nomads Cairns, 341 Lake St, Cairns North QLD; T:(07)40407777, *bookings@ nomadsworld.com/*; $25bed, Kitchen:Y, B'fast:N, WiFi:Y, Pvt.room:Y, Locker:Y, Recep:ltd; Note: activities, not central, arpt pickup, tour desk, laundry, c.c., billiards

Gilligan's Backpackers Hotel & Resort, 57-89 Grafton St, Cairns; T:0740416566, *reservations@ gilligans.com.au/*; $21bed, Kitchen:Y, B'fast:N, WiFi:Y, Pvt.room:Y, Locker:N, Recep:24/7; Note: resto/bar, arpt pickup, bikes, tour desk, laundry, c.c. ok, wh/chair ok

Calypso Inn Backpackers Resort, 5/9 Digger St, Cairns QLD; T:0740310910, *res@ calypsobackpackers.com.au/*; $23bed, Kitchen:Y, B'fast:N, WiFi:$, Pvt. room:Y, Locker:N, Recep:24/7; Note: bar, arpt pickup, bikes, laundry, c.c. ok, pool, billiards, far

Beach House Cairns, 239 Sheridan St., Cairns, Australia; T:+180022922, *cairnsbeachhouse.com.au/*; $18bed, Kitchen:Y, B'fast:Y, WiFi:Y, Pvt.room:Y, Locker:N, Recep:>11p; Note: pool, resto/bar, luggage rm, laundry, c.c. ok, a/c, far, beach

Reef Backpackers, 140 Grafton St, Cairns City QLD; T:0740415255, *info@ reefbackpackers.com/*; $14bed, Kitchen:Y, B'fast:Y, WiFi:Y, Pvt.room:Y, Locker:Y, Recep:ltd; Note: tour desk, laundry, c.c. ok, pool, billiards, safe deposit, a/c

Njoy! Travellers Resort, 141 Sheridan St, Cairns QLD; T:(07)40311088, *info@ njoy.net.au/*; $19bed, Kitchen:Y, B'fast:N, WiFi:$, Pvt.room:Y, Locker:N, Recep:24/7; Note: arpt pickup, pool, wh/chair ok, tour desk, laundry, c.c. ok, billiards

Tropic Days Hostel, 26-28 Bunting St, Cairns QLD; T:0740411521, *info@ tropicdays.com.au/*; $27bed, Kitchen:Y, B'fast:N, WiFi:Y, Pvt.room:Y, Locker:N, Recep:ltd; Note: free WiFi, pool, wh/chair ok, tour desk, laundry, c.c., billiards, far

The Jack Backpackers, Cnr Spence/Sheridan St, Cairns QLD; *thejack.com. au/*, T:0740512490; $19bed, Kitchen:N, B'fast:N, WiFi:N, Pvt.room:Y, Locker:N, Recep:8a>8p; Note: CBD, resto/bar, free meal, laundry, c.c. ok, billiards

The Northern Greenhouse, 117 Grafton St, Cairns QLD; T:(07)40477200; *northern@friendlygroup.com.au*; $26bed, *northerngreenhouse.com.au/*, Kitchen:Y, B'fast:Y, WiFi:Y, Pvt.room:N, Locker:Y, Recep:24/7; Note: bar, free WiFi, pool, wh/chair ok, tour desk, laundry, c.c. ok

Globetrotters International, 154/156 Lake St, Cairns QLD; T:0419744431, *info@ globetrottersinternational.com.au/*; $26bed, Kitchen:Y, B'fast:N, WiFi:Y, Pvt.room:Y, Locker:N, Recep:ltd; Note: pool, tour desk, laundry, c.c. ok, a/c, parking, non-party

Cairns City Backpackers, 274 Draper St, Cairns QLD; T:+61/40516160, *info@ cairnscitybackpackers.com/*; $18bed, Kitchen:Y, B'fast:N, WiFi:Y, Pvt. room:Y, Locker:N, Recep:8a-8p; Note: free meal, tour desk, laundry, c.c. ok, a/c, not central, min. 2 nights

BHA Central, 106 Sheridan St, Cairns QLD; T:0740521818, *info@ bohemiacentral.com.au/*; $21bed, Kitchen:Y, B'fast:Y, WiFi:Y, Pvt.room:Y, Locker:N, Recep:ltd; Note: resto/bar, arpt pickup, pool, laundry, c.c. ok, a/c, luggage room

JJ's Backpackers Hostel, 11-13 Charles St, Cairns QLD; *jjsbackpackers. com/*, T:0740517642, *jjsbackpackers@ledanet.com.au*; $25bed, Kitchen:Y, B'fast:Y, WiFi:Y, Pvt.room:Y, Locker:Y, Recep:ltd; Note: not central, bikes, tour desk, laundry, c.c. ok, pool, luggage room

Castaway's Backpackers, 207 Sheridan St, Cairns QLD; T:(07)40511238, *info@ castawaysbackpackers.com.au/*; $25bed, Kitchen:Y, B'fast:N, WiFi:Y, Pvt. room:Y, Locker:Y, Recep:ltd; Note: tour desk, laundry, c.c. ok, pool, no bunks, a/c, shuttle>town

Caravella Backpackers Cairns City Waterfront, 149 The Esplanade; T:0740512431, *info@ caravella.com.au/*; $23bed, Kitchen:Y, B'fast:N, WiFi:Y, Pvt. room:Y, Locker:N, Recep:>8p; Note: arpt pickup, tour desk, laundry, c.c. ok, billiards, free meal, pool

Corona Backpackers, 72 Grafton St, Cairns QLD; T:0740415288, *info@ coronabackpackers.com.au/*; $20bed, Kitchen:Y, B'fast:N, WiFi:Y, Pvt.room:Y, Locker:N, Recep:8a-7p; Note: laundry, safe deposit, a/c, luggage room, central

Woodduck Backpackers Cairns, 136 Grafton St, Cairns QLD; T:1800152000, *cairns@ woodduck.com.au/*; $20bed, Kitchen:Y, B'fast:Y, WiFi:Y, Pvt.room:N, Locker:Y, Recep:ltd; Note: free meal/WiFi/pickup, laundry, c.c. ok, pool, luggage rm, parking

Bellview Motel and Guest House, 85/87 Esplanade, Cairns QLD; T:0740314377, *stay@ bellviewcairns.com.au/*; $23bed, Kitchen:N, B'fast:N, WiFi:Y, Pvt.room:Y, Locker:N, Recep:24/7; Note: pool, wh/chair ok, tour desk, laundry, c.c. ok, a/c, near lagoon

Global Backpackers Central, 86-88 Lake St, Cairns QLD, T:0740317921

Global Backpakers On The Waterfront, 67-69 The Esplanade, Cairns QLD; T:+61/740311545, *bookings@ globalbackpackerscairns.com.au/*, $21bed, Kitchen:Y, B'fast:N, WiFi:Y, Pvt.room:Y, Locker:N, Recep:ltd; Note: bar, tour desk, laundry, c.c. ok, billiards, luggage rm, a/c, central

CAPE TRIBULATION was named by James Cook, during a period of tribulations in 1770 as his ship hit a reef here. Today it is home to 101 people and borders prime rainforest that only got a paved road within the last few years. That primitive forest is one of its main draws for ecotourism. The other is the Great Barrier Reef, twelve miles out in the ocean. It is located within the Daintree National Park and the Wet Tropics World Heritage area.

www.capetribulation.com.au/

Crocodylus Village, Lot 5 Buchanan Creek Rd, Cow Bay QLD; T:(07)40989166, *info@ daintreecrocodylus.com.au/*; $26bed, Kitchen:Y, B'fast:$, WiFi:Y, Pvt.room:Y, Locker:N, Recep:ltd; Note: billiards, tour desk, laundry, c.c. ok, pool, resto/bar, bike rent

Cape Trib Beach House, Rykers Rd, Cape Tribulation QLD; T:0740980030, *reservations@ capetribbeach.com.au/*; $26bed, Kitchen:Y, B'fast:N, WiFi:Y, Pvt. room:N, Locker:N, Recep:ltd; Note: a/c, resto/bar, wh/chair ok, laundry, pool, billiards, luggage rm

COOLANGATTA is the southernmost component of the tourist conurbation known as Gold Coast and lies on the border of Queensland and New South Wales. If you fly into the glorified Quonset hut known as Gold Coast International Airport, your plane might just cross the county line on takeoff. Coolangatta even has a twin town known as Tweed Heads that sits on the other side of that line. Named for a schooner that wrecked here in 1846, Coolangatta was one of the original settlements on what has now been dubbed by marketing departments as the Gold Coast. There is a fishing fleet, though the area is mainly know for its vacation amenities — beaches, food, and... hostels.
www.visitgoldcoast.com

Coolangatta Sands Hostel, Cnr McLean St/Griffith St, Coolangatta QLD; *coolangattasandshostel.com.au/*, T:0755367472, *hostel@taphouse.com.au;*$30bed, Kitchen:Y, B'fast:Y, WiFi:Y, Pvt.room:Y, Locker:N, Recep:ltd; Note: resto/bar, laundry, billiards, c.c. ok, arpt p-u, a/c, ATM, beach

Komune - Gold Coast, 144-146 Marine Parade, Coolangatta QLD; T:(07)55366764, *info@ komuneresorts.com/*; $36bed, Kitchen:N, B'fast:Y, WiFi:Y, Pvt.room:N, Locker:Y, Recep:ltd; Note: parking, a/c, resto/bar, wh/chair ok, laundry, luggage room, beach

Coolangatta YHA, 230 Coolangatta Rd, Bilinga, Coolangatta QLD; T:0755367644, *booking@ coolangattayha.com/*; $31bed, Kitchen:Y, B'fast:Y, WiFi:Y, Pvt.room:N, Locker:Y, Recep:ltd; Note: wh/chair ok, laundry, pool, billiards, luggage rm, c.c. ok, nr arpt

EMU PARK is a small seaside resort of three thou on the Queensland coast. It is home of the famous Singing Ship Monument. I assume there are some emus, too.
www.emuparkonline.com.au/

Emus Beach Resort, 92 Pattison St, Emu Park QLD; *emusbeachresort.com/*, T:(07)49396111; $31bed, Kitchen:Y, B'fast:N WiFi:Y, Pvt.room:Y, Locker:N Recep:ltd; Note: wh/chair ok, laundry, pool, luggage rm, c.c. ok, bar, forex, far

4) Queensland, Australia

HERVEY BAY (PIALBA/SCARNESS/TORQUAY/URANGAN, etc) is a city on the Queensland coast 180mi/290km north of the capital Brisbane. Amalgamated from a collection of seaside villages, its primary bizniz is tourism. Aside from the beaches, whale watching, Fraser Island and Lady Elliot Island are the main attractions. Indigenous Butchulla people are the original residents of Hervey Bay, before James Cook stopped by in 1770. The rest is history. The town is served by high-speed Tilt Train. Shazam!
www.discoverherveybay.com/

The Friendly Hostel, 182 Torquay Rd, Scarness QLD; *friendlyhostel.com.au/,* T:1800244107; $26bed, Kitchen:Y, B'fast:$, WiFi:Y, Pvt.room:Y, Locker:Y, Recep:ltd; Note: parking, laundry, safe deposit, c.c. ok, a/c, bikes, homey

Flashpackers Hervey Bay, 195 Torquay Terrace, Torquay QLD; T:0741241366, *flashpackersherveybay.com/*; $25bed, Kitchen:Y, B'fast:Y, WiFi:Y, Pvt.room:Y, Locker:N Recep:ltd; Note: wh/chair ok, laundry, pool, luggage rm, c.c. ok, free tour/info

Aussie Woolshed Backpackers Hervey Bay, 181 Torquay Rd, Scarness; *woolshedbackpackers.com.au/,* T:(07)41240677; $23bed, Kitchen:Y, B'fast:$, WiFi:Y, Pvt.room:Y, Locker:Y, Recep:7a-7p; Note: parking, laundry, safe deposit, c.c. ok, a/c, bikes, tour desk, quiet

Colonial Village YHA, 820 Boat Harbour Dr, Urangan QLD; T:0741251844, *herveybay@ yha.com.au/;* $38bed, Kitchen:Y, B'fast:N, WiFi:Y, Pvt.room:Y, Locker:Y, Recep:ltd; Note: parking, wh/chair ok, laundry, pool, luggage $, c.c. ok, tour info

Mango Eco Tourist Hostel, 110 Torquay Road, Hervey Bay, QLD; T:(07)41242832, *mango123@ mangohostel.com/*; $29bed, Kitchen:Y, B'fast:N, WiFi:Y, Pvt.room:Y, Locker:N, Recep:>8p; Note: parking, laundry, tour desk, homey, cozy

Palace Backpackers Hervey Bay, 184 Torquay Road, Scarness QLD; TF:1800063168, *island@ palaceadventures.com.au/*; $26bed, Kitchen:Y, B'fast:N, WiFi:Y, Pvt.room:Y, Locker:Y, Recep:ltd; Note: laundry, pool, billiards, c.c. ok, parking, bikes, Fraser I. tours

MACKAY is a city of some 75,000 on the northern Queensland coast, 600mi/1000km north of Brisbane, and founded on Yuibera traditional lands. It is known as the "sugar capital" of Australia, and mining is also important. Tourism is small but growing, with attractions nearby such as Eungella National Park, the Great Barrier Reef, and the Whitsunday Islands. There is also an arts community, and a Mackay Festival of Arts.
  www.queenslandholidays.com.au

  Gecko's Rest, 34 Sydney St, Mackay QLD; T:(07)49441230, *info@ geckosrest. com.au/*; $31bed, Kitchen:Y, B'fast:N, WiFi:Y, Pvt.room:Y, Locker:N, Recep:>9p; Note: laundry, billiards, luggage rm, c.c. ok, safe deposit, CBD

MAGNETIC ISLAND is a mountainous land of some 20sq.mi/50sq.km and 2100 souls at 5mi/8km off the Queensland coast at Townsville. The island reportedly had a "magnetic" effect on Captain Cook's compass. More than half of the island constitutes a national park, teeming with birds and wildlife. Wulguru people were the original inhabitants, and still hold title to lands here. The island is part of the Great Barrier Reef.
  www.magneticinformer.com.au/

  Base Magnetic Island, 1 Nelly Bay Rd, Magnetic Island QLD; T:0747785777, *magnetic@ stayatbase.com/*; $25bed, Kitchen:Y, B'fast:N, WiFi:Y, Pvt.room:Y, Locker:Y, Recep:ltd; Note: resto/bar, laundry, pool, c.c. ok, billiards, tour desk, arpt p-u, party

  Bungalow Bay Koala Village, 40 Horseshoe Bay Rd, Horseshoe Bay; *hihostels.com/*, T:(07)47785577, *magneticisland@yha.com.au;* $29bed, Kitchen:Y, B'fast:N, WiFi:Y, Pvt.room:Y, Locker:N, Recep:ltd; Note: parking, resto/bar, laundry, pool, tour desk, wildlife park

MAROOCHYDORE is a major commercial area of the Sunshine Coast with many shopping centers in the central business district. There are major surf sport carnivals, and it is a convenient transport hub from which to travel to the rest of Queensland.
  www.queenslandholidays.com.au/destinations/sunshine-coast/

Maroochydore, 24 Schirmann Dr, Maroochydore, Sunshine Coast QLD; T:0754433151, *mail@ yhabackpackers.com/*; $29bed, Kitchen:Y, B'fast:Y, WiFi:Y, Pvt.room:Y, Locker:Y, Recep:ltd; Note: parking, bikes, laundry, pool, billiards, luggage room, c.c. ok, far

Cotton Tree Backpackers, 15 The Esplanade, Maroochydore QLD; T:0754431755, *staff@ cottontreebackpackers.com/*; $24bed, Kitchen:Y, B'fast:N, WiFi:N, Pvt.room:Y, Locker:N, Recep:ltd; Note: laundry, pool, c.c. ok, billiards, tour desk, arpt p-u, beach

MISSION BEACH is a town along the northern Coral Sea in Queensland that comprises what were once separate villages. The "mission" refers to a colony of aborigines that once inhabited the area under collective supervision. Today it is a loosely defined tourist town crawling down the coastline between rainforest and barrier reef. This makes for excellent bird and wildlife viewing. Day trips from Cairns are possible.
www.missionbeachtourism.com/

Absolute Backpackers, 28 Wongaling Beach Rd, Mission Beach QLD; T:0740688317, *info@ absolutebackpackers.com.au/*; $24bed, Kitchen:Y, B'fast:N, WiFi:Y, Pvt.room:Y, Locker:Y, Recep:ltd; Note: laundry, pool, c.c. ok, billiards, bikes, hot tub, long walks

Jackaroo Hostel Mission Beach, 13 Frizelle Rd, Bingil Bay QLD; T:(07)40687137, *missionbeach@ jackaroohostel.com/*; $25bed, Kitchen:Y, B'fast:Y, WiFi:Y, Pvt.room:Y, Locker:N, Recep:ltd; Note: bar, laundry, pool, bike, parking, "treehouse/rainforest"

Scotty's Beach House, 167 Reid Rd, Mission Beach QLD; T:0740688676, *info@ scottysbeachhouse.com.au/*; $23bed, Kitchen:Y, B'fast:N, WiFi:Y, Pvt. room:Y, Locker:Y, Recep:>7p; Note: laundry, pool, c.c. ok, billiards, tour desk, resto/bar, a/c

Mission Beach Retreat, 49 Porter Promenade, Mission Beach QLD; T:0740886229, *stay@ missionbeachretreat.com.au/*; $23bed, Kitchen:Y, B'fast:N,

WiFi:Y, Pvt.room:Y, Locker:N, Recep:ltd; Note: laundry, pool, c.c. ok, a/c, tour desk, luggage room, beach, dog

MOOLOOLABA is a suburb and tourist resort on the Sunshine Coast of Queensland, 100km/60mi north of the state capital Brisbane; it is part of Maroochydore's conurbation.
   www.mooloolabatourism.com.au/

Mooloolaba Beach Backpackers, 75 Brisbane Rd, Mooloolaba QLD; T:0754443399, *info@ mooloolababackpackers.com/*; $29bed, Kitchen:Y, B'fast:Y, WiFi:Y, Pvt.room:Y, Locker:Y, Recep:ltd; Note: laundry, pool, c.c. ok, a/c, luggage room, billiards, long-stays

NOOSA was the designation of a governmental entity that existed until 2008, when it and others were folded into the new "Sunshine Coast," which sounds more like a marketing plan than a town, hmmm... The original inhabitants were the *Undumbi* tribe to the south, the *Dulingbara* to the north, and the *Gabbi Gabbi* to the west. Previous home to gold and timber enterprises, at only 60mi/100km north of Brisbane, tourism today is too easy to avoid, much of it the mass-market variety: Steve Irwin's Australia Zoo, Under Water World marine park, Aussie World, The Buderim Ginger Factory, The Big Pineapple and the Majestic Theatre at Pomona. What, no Disneyland?
   www.visitnoosa.com.au/

Noosa Flashpackers, 102 Pacific Ave, Sunshine Beach QLD; T:(07)54554088, *bookings@ flashpackersnoosa.com/*; $34bed, Kitchen:Y, B'fast:Y, WiFi:Y, Pvt. room:Y, Locker:Y, Recep:ltd; Note: parking, laundry, luggage rm, c.c. ok, a/c, bikes, wh/chair ok, pool

Halse Lodge, 2 Halse Lane, Noosa Heads QLD; *halselodge.com.au/*, T:0754473377, F:1800242567; $31bed, Kitchen:Y, B'fast:N, WiFi:Y, Pvt.room:N, Locker:Y, Recep:ltd; Note: resto/bar, wh/chair ok, laundry, luggage rm, billiards, c.c. ok

4) Queensland, Australia

Nomads Noosa, 44 Noosa Drive, Noosa QLD; T:(07)54473355, *bookings@ nomadsworld.com/*; $28bed, Kitchen:Y, B'fast:N, WiFi:Y, Pvt.room:N, Locker:N, Recep:ltd; Note: resto/bar, pool, laundry, tour desk, billiards, c.c. ok, parking, shuttle

Dolphins Beachhouse, 14 Duke St, Sunshine Bch, Noosa, Sunshine Coast; TF:1800454456, *info@ dolphinsbeachhouse.com.au/*; $29bed, Kitchen:Y, B'fast:N, WiFi:Y, Pvt.room:Y, Locker:N, Recep:ltd; Note: pool, laundry, tour desk, billiards, c.c. ok, parking, safe dep, a/c

PORT DOUGLAS lies in far north Queensland, home to 5000 and vacation spot to many more. As with other towns in the area, the attractions are the Great Barrier Reef in the water and the rainforest on land. The town itself has many amenities and events, including the Port Douglas Carnivale in May, and the Beer Festival, Go Troppo Arts Festival, and The Sunset in the Park Music Festival, all in October.
www.pddt.com.au/

Parrotfish Lodge, 37 Warner St, Port Douglas QLD; *parrotfishlodge.com/*, T:(07)40995011; $29bed, Kitchen:Y, B'fast:Y, WiFi:Y, Pvt.room:Y, Locker:N, Recep:ltd; Note: resto/bar, wh/chair ok, bikes, pool, billiards, c.c. ok, parking

Port O'Call Eco Lodge, Craven Close, Port Douglas QLD; T:(07)40995422, *info@ portocall.com.au/*; $40bed, Kitchen:Y, B'fast:$, WiFi:Y, Pvt.room:N, Locker:Y, Recep:ltd; Note: arpt pickup, resto/bar, wh/chair ok, pool, luggage rm, billiards, c.c. ok

Dougies Backpackers Resort, 111 Davidson St, Port Douglas QLD; *dougies. com.au/*, T:0740996200; $24bed, Kitchen:Y, B'fast:N, WiFi:Y, Pvt.room:Y, Locker:Y, Recep:ltd; Note: bikes, resto/bar, wh/chair ok, pool, luggage rm, billiards, c.c. ok

RAINBOW BEACH is a coastal town of a thousand people in southern Queensland 150 mi/240km from Brisbane. It is named for the multi-colored sand dunes surrounding, caused by minerals within, the mining of such once being the town's main industry. Now it's tourism, with the Great Sandy National Park and ferries to Fraser Island.

www.ourrainbowbeach.com.au/

Pippies Beachhouse, 22 Spectrum St, Rainbow Beach QLD; T:(07)54868503, *bookings@ pippiesbeachhouse.com/*; $23bed, Kitchen:Y, B'fast:Y, WiFi:Y, Pvt. room:Y, Locker:N, Recep:ltd; Note: pool, luggage rm, c.c. ok, parking, tour desk, laundry, a/c

Frasers On Rainbow Beach, 18 Spectrum St, Rainbow Beach QLD; T:(07)54868885, *adventures@ frasersonrainbow.com/*; $26bed, Kitchen:Y, B'fast:N, WiFi:Y, Pvt.room:Y, Locker:N, Recep:ltd; Note: resto/bar, pool, luggage rm, billiards, c.c. ok, tour desk, laundry

ROCKHAMPTON, "beef capital of Australia," is a town of some 60,000 on the Queensland coast 370mi/600km north of Brisbane, slightly south of the Capricorn Coast, and traditional home to the Darumbal people. Born in a gold rush, wool and agricultural products proved to be more stable exports. The Multicultural Festival, the Village Festival of Arts and Music, and Big River Jazz are popular events.

www.sunzine.net/rockhampton/rockhampton-city.html

Rockhampton Backpackers YHA, 60 Macfarlane St, Berserker QLD; T:0749275288, *rockhamptonyha@ westnet.com.au/*; $23bed, Kitchen:Y, B'fast:N, WiFi:Y, Pvt.room:Y, Locker:Y, Recep:ltd; Note: wh/chair ok, pool, luggage rm, billiards, c.c. ok, parking, laundry, a/c

SURFERS' PARADISE is one of the component parts of Gold Coast City south of Brisbane. An urban beach, 'Surfers' is characterized by high-rise buildings and shopping malls. There is a festival of local music, food, film, fashion, and art every March and April. Surf's good, I hear.

www.surfersparadise.com/

Islander Backpacker Resort, 6 Beach Rd, Surfers Paradise QLD; TF:1800074393, T:0755388000, *res@ islander.com.au/*; $28bed, Kitchen:Y,

4) Queensland, Australia

B'fast:N, WiFi:Y, Pvt.room:Y, Locker:Y, Recep:24/7; Note: resto/bar, billiards, tour desk, pool, c.c. ok, lift, luggage $, safe dep

Gold Coast Intl Backpackers, 28 Hamilton Ave, Surfers Paradise QLD; *goldcoastbackpackers.com.au/,* T:(07)55925888; $26bed, Kitchen:Y, B'fast:N, WiFi:Y, Pvt.room:Y, Locker:N, Recep:>10p; Note: free WiFi, bar, tour desk, laundry, c.c. ok, billiards, central

Trekkers Backpackers Resort, 22 White St, Southport QLD; T:(07)55915616, *info@ trekkersbackpackers.com.au/*; $26bed, Kitchen:Y, B'fast:Y, WiFi:Y, Pvt. room:Y, Locker:N, Recep:ltd; Note: billiards, laundry, c.c. ok, pool, parking, luggage $, safe dep

Sleeping Inn Surfers Backpackers, 22 Peninsular Dr, Surfers Paradise QLD; *sleepinginn.com.au/,* T:(07)55924455; $23bed, Kitchen:Y, B'fast:N, WiFi:Y, Pvt.room:Y, Locker:N, Recep:ltd; Note: free WiFi, billiards, laundry, c.c. ok, pool, parking, wh/chair ok

Surfers Paradise B'packers Resort, 2837 Gold Coast Hwy, Surfers QLD; *surfersparadisebackpackers.com.au/,* T:07755924677, *spbr@bigpond. net.au;* $30bed, Kitchen:Y, B'fast:N, WiFi:Y, Pvt.room:N, Locker:N, Recep:24/7; Note: free WiFi, resto/bar, billiards, tour desk, pool, c.c. ok, luggage rm

Backpackers In Paradise, 40 Peninsular Dr, Surfers Paradise QLD; *backpackersinparadise.com/*, TF:1800268621; $19bed, Kitchen:Y, B'fast:N, WiFi:Y, Pvt.room:Y, Locker:Y, Recep:>9p; Note: billiards, laundry, c.c. ok, pool, bar, safe dep, c.c. ok, central

TOWNSVILLE is the unofficial capital and one of the larger cities of North Queensland, 220mi/350km south of Cairns, and with a population of over 200,000 in the greater metro area. Wulgurukaba and Bindal are among the groups that previously inhabited the area. There is a historic waterfront and several parks. The area is prone to cyclones. The population is young, and there is plenty of entertainment.
www.townsvilleholidays.info/

Civic Guest House Backpackers Hostel, 262 Walker St, Townsville QLD; T:074771538, *info@ civicguesthousetownsville.com.au/*; $25bed, Kitchen:Y, B'fast:N, WiFi:Y, Pvt.room:Y, Locker:N, Recep:8a/8p; Note: bus/ferry pickup, tour desk, laundry, luggage rm, c.c. ok, safe deposit

Foreign Exchange Accom-Beachside, Cnr Eyre/Leichhardt Sts, N. Ward QLD; *foreignexchangeaccommodation.com.au/*, T:0747716878; $25bed, Kitchen:Y, B'fast:N, WiFi:Y, Pvt.room:Y, Locker:N, Recep:8a>7p; Note: luggage rm, billiards, c.c. ok, parking, laundry, safe dep, a/c, bikes

Adventurers Resort, 79 Palmer St, Townsville QLD; *adventurersresort. com/*, T:0747211522, *adventurersresort@hotmail.com*; $25bed, Kitchen:N, B'fast:N, WiFi:Y, Pvt.room:Y, Locker:N, Recep:>8p; Note: resto, pool, luggage rm, billiards, c.c. ok, parking, laundry, a/c, basic

Globetrotters Townsville, 121 Flinders St, Townsville QLD; T:0747715000, *info@ globetrottersaustralia.com/*; $29bed, Kitchen:Y, B'fast:N, WiFi:Y, Pvt. room:Y, Locker:?, Recep:24/7; Note: wkly rates, nr ferry, CBD, club strip, pool, basic, new mgmt

5) South Australia

ADELAIDE has a population of over a million people, making it the fifth-largest city in Australia. In addition it is the capital of the state of South Australia, built for that purpose, in fact. The area was originally the home of the aboriginal Kaurna people, a group which continues to survive in limited numbers. The city was built in a grid pattern with wide boulevards, parks, and a ring road. The climate is a warm Mediterranean one, with wet winters. It long had a reputation as the "city of churches," but these days it's a city of festivals, especially the Adelaide Festival, which includes the Adelaide Cabaret Festival, Adelaide Film Festival, Adelaide Festival of Ideas, Adelaide Writers' Week, and WOMADelaide, the world music event.

Sights, tourist destinations, and landmarks include The Art Gallery of South Australia, the South Australian Museum and State Library of South Australia. The Adelaide Botanic Garden, National Wine Centre and Tandanya National Aboriginal Cultural Institute are in the East End of the city. In the back of the State Library is the Migration Museum. Contemporary art venues include theContemporary Art Centre of South Australia, in addition to the Adelaide Festival Centre. It is also South Australia's wine capital; sounds like a party. Its livability rating is high.

www.cityofadelaide.com.au

Our House Backpackers, 33 Gilbert Place, Adelaide SA; T:(08)84104788, *info@ ourhousebackpackers.com/*; $25bed, Kitchen:Y, B'fast:Y, WiFi:Y, Pvt. room:Y, Locker:Y, Recep:ltd; Note: billiards, tour desk, laundry, c.c. ok, central, wh/chair ok, bar, lift

Backpack Oz, 144 Wakefield St, Adelaide SA; T:(08)82233551, *enquiries@ backpackoz.com.au/*; $27bed, Kitchen:Y, B'fast:Y, WiFi:Y, Pvt.room:Y, Locker:Y, Recep:>10p; Note: free WiFi, bar, tour desk, safe dep, c.c., a/c, bikes, parking, laundry

Glenelg Beach Hostel, 1/5-7 Moseley St, Glenelg SA; T:(08)83760007, *enquiries@ glenelgbeachhostel.com.au/*; $29bed, Kitchen:Y, B'fast:Y, WiFi:Y, Pvt. room:Y, Locker:N, Recep:ltd; Note: free WiFi, bar, tour desk, c.c. ok, bikes, parking, beach, central

Adelaide's Shakespeare Intl Backpackers, 123 Waymouth St, Adelaide SA; TF:1800556889, *info@ shakeys.com.au/*; $28bed, Kitchen:Y, B'fast:$, WiFi:$, Pvt.room:Y, Locker:Y, Recep:ltd; Note: laundry, c.c. ok, central, wh/chair ok, bar, luggage room

Adelaide Motel & Backpackers, 262 Hindley St, Adelaide SA; T:(08)82319524, *adelaidemotelandbackpackers.com/*; $21bed, Kitchen:N, B'fast:Y, WiFi:Y, Pvt.room:Y, Locker:N, Recep:ltd; Note: laundry, c.c., free WiFi, free tour/info, bar, luggage room

Adelaide Travellers Inn Backpackers Hostel, 220 Hutt St, Adelaide SA; TF:1800666237, *bookings@ nomadsworld.com/*; $27bed, Kitchen:Y, B'fast:N, WiFi:Y, Pvt.room:Y, Locker:N, Recep:ltd; Note: tour desk, c.c. ok, bikes, parking, luggage room, laundry

Blue Galah Backpackers Hostel, 1/62 King William St, Adelaide SA; T:(08)82319295, *info@ bluegalah.com.au/*; $28bed, Kitchen:Y, B'fast:Y, WiFi:Y, Pvt.room:Y, Locker:N, Recep:>10p; Note: wh/chair ok, c.c. ok, billiards, tour desk, bar, luggage room, central

Sunny's Adelaide Backpacker Hostel, 139 Franklin St, Adelaide SA; T:(08)82312430, *stay@ sunnys.com.au/*; $22bed, Kitchen:Y, B'fast:Y, WiFi:Y, Pvt.room:Y, Locker:N, Recep:24/7; Note: tour desk, c.c. ok, bikes, parking, luggage room, laundry, central

KANGAROO ISLAND is Australia's third-largest, 1700sq.mi/4400sq.km, and lies off the South Australia coast 70mi/110km southwest of Adelaide. Aboriginals once lived here, before rising sea levels made it an island. The European sealers came in 1802. The island specializes in rock lobster and Ligurian bee honey. Parks and nature draw tourists. Over 4000 people live here permanently.
www.kangaroo-island-au.com/

Kangaroo I. Central Backpackers, 19 Murray St, Kingscote, Kangaroo I; *kicentralbackpackers.com/*, T:0400197231, *ki_hostel@yahoo.com.au*; $26bed, Kitchen:Y, B'fast:N, WiFi:Y, Pvt.room:Y, Locker:N, Recep:24/7; Note: parking, wh/chair ok, laundry, luggage rm

MOUNT GAMBIER is the second largest city of the state of South Australia with 25,000 inhabitants, and is situated near the coast and the Victoria border. The mountain is an extinct volcano. The area is famous for limestone formations, cave diving and Blue Lake, with ever-changing water color.
www.mountgambiertourism.com.au

The Old Mt. Gambier Gaol, 25 Margaret St, Mt. G, SA, *hmgetaway.com. au/*, T:0887230032, *administration@theoldmountgambiergaol.com.au*; $27bed, Kitchen:Y, B'fast:N, WiFi:Y, Pvt.room:Y, Locker:N, Recep:ltd; Note: parking, wh/chair ok, laundry, arpt pickup, billiards, c.c. ok, parking

6) Tasmania

BRIDPORT is a small tourist town in Tasmania that features aquatic activities, estuary life, and… golf. Choose your pleasure. There is a ferry to Flinders Island.

www.about-australia.com/location/tasmania/bridport/

Bridport Seaside Lodge, 47 Main St, Bridport TAS; *bridportseasidelodge. com/*, T:(03)63561585; $29bed, Kitchen:Y, B'fast:N, WiFi:N, Pvt.room:Y, Locker:Y, Recep:ltd; Note: parking, c.c. ok, luggage room, wh/chair ok, laundry, sea view

HOBART is the state capital and largest city of Tasmania, the large island that lies to the south of Australia, and presumably at one time attached to it during times of lower water levels. At a latitude of 42°52′S, it serves as a base for Australia's Antarctic operations. It used to be a center for whaling and sealing, an industry no longer practiced in Oz. Even though Hobart's economy is limited, its livability index is high. Tourism rocks, too, based on cruise ships, nature, arts, and history. There is a vibrant music and nightlife culture, and a massive weekly market in Salamanca Place. Wine's good.

www.discovertasmania.com/

Transit Backpackers, 251 Liverpool St, Hobart TAS; *transitbackpackers.com/*, T:(03)62312400; $20bed, Kitchen:Y, B'fast:N, WiFi:Y, Pvt.room:Y, Locker:N, Recep:ltd; Note: wh/chair ok, laundry, luggage rm, c.c. ok, tour info, nr CBD

The Pickled Frog, 281 Liverpool St, Hobart TAS; T:0362347977, *info@ thepickledfrog.com/*; $25bed, Kitchen:Y, B'fast:N, WiFi:Y, Pvt.room:Y, Locker:Y, Recep:ltd; Note: laundry, bar, billiards, luggage rm, c.c. ok, parking, bikes, safe dep

LAUNCESTON is the second-largest city in Tasmania, located north-centrally and home to over 100,000. Tasmanian aboriginals occupied the area until the arrival of Europeans in 1798, who then engaged in sheep-raising and mineral extraction. Tourism is now important, with natural attractions the main draw; culture and history, too.

www.launceston.tas.gov.au/lcc/

Arthouse Hostel, 20 Lindsay St, Launceston, TAS; T:0363330222, *bookings@ arthousehostel.com.au/*; $24bed, Kitchen:Y, B'fast:N, WiFi:Y, Pvt. room:N, Locker:N, Recep:>9p; Note: parking, wh/chair ok, laundry, luggage rm, c.c. ok, historic bldg

7) Victoria

APOLLO BAY is the original home of the Gadubanud or King Parrot people of the Cape Otway coast, along the edge of the Barham River and on the Great Ocean Road, in southwestern Victoria, Australia,. Originally a whaling station accessible only from the sea, it later drew timber-cutters and sawmills, then farmers. Today it has a population of almost 2000 and plays host to the annual Apollo Bay Music Festival and the Great Ocean Sports Festival. Economically it is an important fishing port, in addition to tourist center. Melbourne is only a couple hours away.

www.visitvictoria.com/

Apollo Bay Backpackers Lodge, 23 Pascoe St, Apollo Bay VIC; T:(03)52377850, *apollobaybackpackerslodge.com.au/*; $27bed, Kitchen:Y, B'fast:Y,

WiFi:Y, Pvt.room:Y, Locker:N, Recep:ltd; Note: luggage room, tour desk, laundry, c.c. ok, parking, a/c, center

Apollo Bay Eco YHA, 5 Pascoe St, Apollo Bay, Australia VIC; T:0352377899, *apollobay@ yha.com.au/*; $37bed, Kitchen:N, B'fast:N, WiFi:N, Pvt.room:Y, Locker:N, Recep:10a>5p; Note: parking, c.c. ok, central, wh/chair ok, laundry

ECHUCA has a population of over 12,000, and is located at the junction of the Murray, Camaspe, and Goulburn Rivers. As such it was a thriving river port in the 19th century, after beginning life as a ferry crossing. Today there is a bridge across the river and the main business is tourism, for here resides the world's largest collection of operating paddle steamers. You heard it here first.

www.echucamoama.com/

Echuca Backpackers, 410 High St, Echuca VIC; *backpackersechuca.com.au/*, T:(03)54807866; $26bed, Kitchen:Y, B'fast:N, WiFi:Y, Pvt.room:Y, Locker:Y, Recep:ltd; Note: parking, c.c. ok, laundry, a/c

HALLS GAP is a small town adjacent to GRAMPIANS NATIONAL PARK (Gariwerd), and is the service center for it. Brambuk is the aboriginal cultural center. The park itself has many rock art sites and great natural beauty.

www.visithallsgap.com.au/

Grampians Eco YHA, 14-16 Grampians Road, Halls Gap VIC; T:(03)53564544, *grampians@ yha.com.au/*; $35bed, Kitchen:Y, B'fast:N, WiFi:Y, Pvt.room:Y, Locker:Y, Recep:ltd; Note: wh/chair ok, c.c. ok, parking, laundry

MELBOURNE is the capital and largest city in the state of Victoria, and, with over four million people, the second-largest in Australia. The city was founded in 1835 and became a wealthy city — and state capital — during the gold rush of 1851. Prior to that, the Wurundjeri, Boonwurrung and Wathaurong people inhabited the area for tens of thousands of years. They lost all that within the first five years of European settlement. In 1851 the longest continuously inhabited Chinese settlement in the western world was established. By the 1880's Melbourne was the richest city in the world. During this period much of the city's finest architecture was created, including some that exist to this day: Parliament House, the Treasury Building, the Old Melbourne Jail, the State Library, Supreme Court, General Post Office, Government House, Customs House, Melbourne Town Hall, St Patrick's cathedral and Queen Victoria Market. All booms go bust, though, so after the banking crisis of 1893 the city went into a severe decline.

With Melbourne the old-industry "rust belt" center of Australia and with a national mentality of urban sprawl, the 20th century was all about Sydney's assuming primacy, what with the governmental seat long since removed to Canberra. That's changing now, with progressive politics and a growth plan embodied in the 'Melbourne @ Five Million' strategy that emphasizes sustainability. Melbourne has always been known as a garden city; just within the urban area are Mornington Peninsula National Park, Port Phillip Heads Marine National Park, Point Nepean National Park in the south east, Organ Pipes National Park to the north, and Dandenong Ranges National Park to the east. The cultural offerings span all genres and are best sampled in its free festivals: Moomba, the Melbourne International Arts Festival, Melbourne International Film Festival, Melbourne International Comedy Festival and the Melbourne Fringe Festival. Then there's the alternative cultural scene—street, rave, etc. Better go see for yourself. Melbourne rates highly on most world livability indices.

www.visitmelbourne.com/

Space Hotel, 380 Russell St, Melbourne VIC; T:+61/396623888, *stay@ spacehotel.com.au/*; $31bed, Kitchen:Y, B'fast:N, WiFi:Y, Pvt.room:Y, Locker:Y, Recep:24/7; Note: resto/bar, wh/chair ok, luggage rm, tour desk, laundry, a/c, center

Nomads Melbourne, 198 A'Beckett St, Melbourne VIC, T:(03)93284383;

Nomads World, 2 Spencer St, Melbourne VIC, T:(03)96201022; TF:1800NOMADS, *bookings@ nomadsworld.com/*; $24bed, Kitchen:Y, B'fast:N, WiFi:Y, Pvt.room:Y, Locker:N, Recep:24/7; Note: bar, billiards, luggage rm, tour desk, laundry, near station, free carbs

7) Victoria

Hotel Discovery, 167 Franklin St, Melbourne VIC; T:+61/393297525, *reservations@ hoteldiscovery.com.au/*, $28bed, Kitchen:Y, B'fast:Y, WiFi:Y, Pvt.room:Y, Locker:N, Recep:24/7; Note: free WiFi, CBD, arpt p-u, resto/bar, wh/chair ok, free tour/info

Melbourne Metro YHA, 78 Howard St, Melbourne VIC; T:+61/393268427, *melbmetro@ yha.com.au/*; $37bed, Kitchen:Y, B'fast:N, WiFi:$, Pvt.room:Y, Locker:Y, Recep:24/7; Note: lift, wh/chair ok, tour desk, laundry, c.c. ok, bike rent, ATM

Urban Central Backpackers, 334 City Rd, Melbourne VIC; T:(03)96933700, *stayplay@ urbancentral.com.au/*; $34bed, Kitchen:Y, B'fast:Y, WiFi:Y, Pvt. room:Y, Locker:Y, Recep:24/7; Note: resto/bar, wh/chair ok, luggage rm, tour desk, laundry, billiards

The Nunnery, 116 Nicholson St, Fitzroy VIC; TF:1800032635, *info@ nunnery.com.au/*; $31bed, Kitchen:Y, B'fast:Y, WiFi:$, Pvt.room:Y, Locker:N, Recep:ltd; Note: luggage rm, tour desk, laundry, TV, games, c.c. ok, free eats

Melbourne Central YHA, 562 Flinders St, Melbourne VIC; T:(03)96212523, *melbcentral@ yha.com.au/*; $44bed, Kitchen:Y, B'fast:$, WiFi:Y, Pvt.room:N, Locker:N, Recep:24/7; Note: bar, lift, wh/chair ok, tour desk, laundry, c.c. ok, big, central

St. Kilda Beach House, 109 Barkly St, Kilda VIC;T:(03)9525337, *info@ stkildabeachhouse.com/*; $31bed, Kitchen:Y, B'fast:Y, WiFi:Y, Pvt.room:Y, Locker:Y, Recep:24/7; Note: resto/bar, lift, wh/chair ok, tour desk, laundry, c.c. ok, billiards, a/c

Base Melbourne St Kilda, 17 Carlisle St, Kilda VIC; T:(03)85986200, *melbourne@ stayatbase.com/*; $31bed, Kitchen:Y, B'fast:$, WiFi:Y, Pvt.room:Y, Locker:Y, Recep:24/7; Note: bar, billiards, wh/chair ok, tour desk, laundry, c.c. ok, parking

The Ritz for Backpackers, 169B Fitzroy St, Kilda VIC; T:(03)95253501, *info@ ritzbackpackers.com/*; $23bed, Kitchen:Y, B'fast:Y, WiFi:Y, Pvt.room:Y,

Locker:N, Recep:24/7; Note: free WiFi & pancakes!, resto/bar, tour desk, laundry, c.c. ok, billiards

King Street Backpackers, 197 King St, Melbourne VIC; T:0396701111, *info@ kingstreetbackpackers.com.au/*; $29bed, Kitchen:Y, B'fast:Y, WiFi:Y, Pvt. room:N, Locker:Y, Recep:24/7; Note: wh/chair ok, tour desk, laundry, c.c. ok, TV, safe dep, nr bus/train

Collingwood Backpackers, 137 Johnston St, Collingwood, Melbourne VIC; T:0420804208, *beds@ collingwoodbackpackers.com/*; $30bed, Kitchen:Y, B'fast:N, WiFi:Y, Pvt.room:N, Locker:Y, Recep:24/7; Note: weeky rates, luggage room, c.c. ok, laundry, safe deposit, smoke

Elizabeth Hostel, 490 Elizabeth St, Melbourne VIC; *elizabethhostel.com.au/*, T:0396631685, *elizabethhostel@hotmail.com;* $31bed, Kitchen:Y, B'fast:N, WiFi:Y, Pvt.room:Y, Locker:Y, Recep:24/7; Note: free WiFi, laundry, c.c. ok, TV, central

Lords Lodge, 204 Punt Road, Prahran VIC; *lordslodge.com.au/*, T:(03)95105658; $25bed, Kitchen:Y, B'fast:N, WiFi:Y, Pvt.room:Y, Locker:Y, Recep:ltd; Note: historical mansion, long-stays, c.c. ok, laundry, free WiFi

Melbourne Connection, 205 King St, Melbourne VIC; T:(03)96424464, *melbourneconnection.com/*; $29bed, Kitchen:Y, B'fast:N, WiFi:Y, Pvt.room:N, Locker:Y, Recep:ltd; Note: luggage room, c.c. ok, laundry, tour desk, a/c, basic

The Spencer Backpackers, 475 Spencer St, West Melbourne VIC; *spencerbackpackers.com.au/*, T:0393297755, *hotelspencer@hotkey.net.au;* $26bed, Kitchen:Y, B'fast:N, WiFi:Y, Pvt.room:Y, Locker:N, Recep:ltd; Note: resto/bar, luggage room, c.c. ok, laundry, tour desk, parking, basic

Elephant Backpacker, 250 Flinders St, Melbourne VIC; T:0396542616, *reception@ elephantbackpacker.com.au/*; $21bed, Kitchen:Y, B'fast:N, WiFi:Y, Pvt. room:Y, Locker:Y, Recep:24/7; Note: free tour/info, near station, cheap, basic

Coffee Palace Backpackers, 24 Grey St, Melbourne VIC; T:0395345283, *info@ coffeepalacebackpackers.com.au/*; $29bed, Kitchen:Y, B'fast:Y, WiFi:Y, Pvt.

room:Y, Locker:N, Recep:24/7; Note: bar, billiards, laundry, c.c. ok, parking, not central, basic

Back of Chapel Backpackers, 50 Green St, Windsor VIC; T:(03)95215338, *info@ backofchapel.com/*; $27bed, Kitchen:Y, B'fast:Y, WiFi:Y, Pvt.room:Y, Locker:Y, Recep:>5p; Note: resto/bar, wh/chair ok, tour desk, laundry, c.c. ok, central, free WiFi

PHILIP ISLAND lies 90mi/145km southeast of Melbourne on Westernport Bay, home to almost 10,000 permanent residents, and quadruple that number in summer. It is a major tourist destination, with mild weather and nature the big draws. That includes the Penguin Parade at Phillip Island Nature Park. Take a camera. Surf's good, too.
www.visitmelbourne.com/Regions/Phillip-Island.aspx

The Island Accommodation, 10-12 Phillip Island Rd, Philip Island VIC; T:0359566123, *info@ theislandaccommodation.com.au/*; $36bed, Kitchen:Y, B'fast:N, WiFi:Y, Pvt.room:Y, Locker:Y, Recep:ltd; Note: wh/chair ok, laundry, billiards, c.c. ok, parking, a/c, penguins

PORT CAMPBELL is a coastal town in Victoria, home to a few hundred, and serving tourists visiting the Twelve Apostles and the Port Campbell National Park. The park features limestone formations, shipwrecks, and wildlife, mainly birds. It is on the Great Ocean Road.
www.travelvictoria.com.au/portcampbell/

Port Campbell Hostel, 18 Tregea St, Port Campbell VIC; T:0355986305, *reception@ portcampbellhostel.com.au/*; $26bed, Kitchen:Y, B'fast:N, WiFi:Y, Pvt. room:N, Locker:N, Recep:ltd; Note: wh/chair ok, laundry, c.c. ok, parking, luggage room

PRINCETOWN is a village on the GREAT OCEAN ROAD, with almost 500 inhabitants on a busy New Year's Day. There are estuaries and wetlands, and the Twelve Apostles (rock formations) are only six clicks away, but the main attraction is

the road itself. Officially designated B100, this is 150mi/240km of paved road hugging the stunning southeastern Victorian coastline between Torquay and Warnambool.
www.visitvictoria.com/Regions/Great-Ocean-Road.aspx

The 13th Apostle, 5 Post Office Rd, Princetown VIC; *the13thapostle.com.au/*, T:(03)55988062, *the13thapostle@live.com*; $26bed, Kitchen:Y, B'fast:Y, WiFi:N, Pvt.room:Y, Locker:N, Recep:ltd; Note: tour desk, parking, near pub/store

WARMAMBOOL is a small city of 34,000 on the coast of Victoria 165mi/265km southwest of Melbourne and on the western end of the Great Ocean Road. It was an important port in the Victoria gold rush. Agriculture is the mainstay now, but tourism is important, featuring shipwreck artefacts, whale-watching, and beaches.
www.travelvictoria.com.au/warrnambool/

Warrnambool Beach Backpackers, 17 Stanley St, Warrnambool VIC; T:0355624874, *info@   beachbackpackers.com.au/*; $28bed, Kitchen:Y, B'fast:N, WiFi:Y, Pvt.room:Y, Locker:Y, Recep:ltd; Note: resto/bar, luggage rm, billiards, c.c. ok, tour info, laundry, basic

8) West Australia

ALBANY is on the west coast south of Perth, and was originally the home of the Noongar people. More recently it became known as a deepwater port and gateway to the gold fields. Now it is better known for tourism, with historic sights that include the Museum, the Albany Convict Gaol, the Princess Royal Fortress, and Patrick Taylor Cottage, oldest dwelling in Western Australia.
www.westernaustralia.com/

Albany Backpackers, Stirling Terrace, Albany WA; *albanybackpackers.com. au/*, T:(08)98418848, *abp@westnet.com.au*; $29bed, Kitchen:Y, B'fast:Y, WiFi:Y,

Pvt.room:Y, Locker:N, Recep:ltd; Note: parking, billiards, c.c. ok, bikes, luggage room, laundry, central

BROOME is a town of some 15K on the far northwestern coast, home to pearls and tourists. In tourist season the population triples. These are the traditional lands of the Yawuru people. Others came later, mostly to work in the pearl industry. The town's Japanese cemetery is for the 919 Japanese divers who lost their lives working in the industry. Shinju Matsuri (Japanese for 'festival of the pearl') celebrates the Asian-influenced culture brought here by the pearling industry. Ironically Broome was attacked at least four times by Japanese aircraft during the Second World War. Today Broome is something of a boom town, based on mining and tourism. Broome is surrounded by water. Town Beach on Roebuck Bay features an awesome natural phenomenon on 'Staircase to the Moon' nights. Clothing is optional on Cable Beach.
  www.broomevisitorcentre.com.au/

Kimberley Klub, 62 Frederick St, (opp. Toyota & BP) Broome WA; TF:1800004345, *info@ kimberleyklub.com/*; $30bed, Kitchen:N, B'fast:N, WiFi:Y, Pvt.room:Y, Locker:Y, Recep:24/7; Note: billiards, tour desk, laundry, c.c. ok, wh/chair ok, pool, luggage rm

Roebuck Bay Backpackers, Chinatown, Carnarvorn St, Broome, WA; *roebuckbayhotel.com.au/*, T:0891922390, *reservations@roey.com.au*; $21bed, Kitchen:Y, B'fast:N, WiFi:Y, Pvt.room:N, Locker:N, Recep:ltd; Note: parking, a/c, resto/bar, wh/chair ok, laundry, pool, billiards

Cable Beach Backpackers, 12 Sanctuary Rd, Broome WA; T:0891935511, *mail@ cablebeachbackpackers.com/*; $26bed, Kitchen:Y, B'fast:N, WiFi:Y, Pvt.room:N, Locker:N, Recep:ltd; Note: parking, a/c, bar, laundry, pool, billiards, luggage room, arpt p-u

BUNBURY is the third largest city in the state of West Australia, situated some 108mi/175 km south of the capital at Perth, and home to over 30,000 people. The economy is based on farming, mining, and timber. It is served by rail and

bus. Tourist attractions include the Dolphin Discovery Center, the Big Swamp mango reserve, and the Tuart Forest National Park.
www.mybunbury.com/

Wander Inn Bunbury Backpackers, 16 Clifton St, Bunbury WA; T:1800039032, *book@ bunburybackpackers.com.au/*; $29bed, Kitchen:Y, B'fast:Y, WiFi:Y, Pvt.room:Y, Locker:N, Recep:ltd; Note: parking, c.c. ok, laundry, billiards

Dolphin Retreat Bunbury, 14 Wellington St, Bunbury WA; T:0897924690, *info@ dolphinretreatbunbury.com.au/*; $28bed, Kitchen:Y, B'fast:Y, WiFi:Y, Pvt. room:Y, Locker:Y, Recep:ltd; Note: prkng, c.c. ok, laundry, billiards, a/c, long-stays

EXMOUTH sits on the far northwest coast of Australia, 1300km/800 mi north of Perth and 3400km/2100mi southwest of Darwin. It owes its existence to a nearby American military base which has operated there since WWII and for which Exmouth serves as a supply depot. Today tourism from the beach and Cape Range National Park is more important and cause the town to swell from 2000 to 6000 in high season.
www.exmouthwa.com.au/

Exmouth Cape Holiday Park, 3 Truscott Crescent, Exmouth WA; T:(08)99491101, *exmouth@ aspenparks.com.au/*; $32bed, Kitchen:Y, B'fast:N, WiFi:Y, Pvt.room:Y, Locker:N, Recep:>6p; Note: parking, laundry, pool, c.c. ok

Potshot Hotel Resort, 1 Murat Rd, Exmouth WA; *potshotresort.com/*, T:(08)99491200, *potshotresort@bigpond.com*; $31bed, Kitchen:Y, B'fast:N, WiFi:Y, Pvt.room:N, Locker:N, Recep:ltd; Note: parking, a/c, resto/bar, laundry, pool, luggage rm, c.c. ok, safe dep

FREMANTLE is the harbor for Perth and a city of 25,000 in its own right. Traditional inhabitants are the Whadjuk Noongar, people who still use the area for ceremonies. It came into commercial prominence as a supply port for the 19th century gold rush. As such it has an architectural heritage lacking in most of West Australia. That includes Edwardian, Georgian, and Victorian styles, and the Fremantle prison which is now a UNESCO world heritage site. The Fremantle Arts Centre and Fremantle Markets are less imposing but almost equally significant.

www.fremantlewesternaustralia.com/

Sundancer Backpackers Resort, 80 High St, Fremantle WA; *sundancer-resort.joyeurs.com/*, T:0893366080, *info@sundancebackpackers.com;* $29bed, Kitchen:Y, B'fast:$, WiFi:Y, Pvt.room:N, Locker:Y, Recep:24/7; Note: laundry, pool, billiards, luggage rm, c.c. ok, bar, parking, big, central

KALGOORLIE is one of the few cities in Western Australia that is not on the ocean. That's because of the gold, mate. Gold was discovered in 1898 and has been a major industry ever since. The town's population was about 30,000 in 1903 and that's what it is today. With Perth almost 400mi/650km away, this is the largest town for many hundreds of miles in any direction. The Wild West brothels have become museums, though, and the prostitutes have become legends. The big deal these days is the Super Pit, almost a cubic mile of hole, blasted out of the earth for the purpose of teasing out its gold. Visitors can watch the blasts; or they can get drunk in town, flirting with the Kalgoorlie Skimpies. The city is served by bus, train, and plane. The originals are Wangai people.

www.kalgoorlietourism.com/

Golddust Backpackers, 192 Hay Street, Kalgoorlie WA; T:61/890913737, *kalgoorlie@ yha.com.au/*; $35bed, Kitchen:Y, B'fast:N, WiFi:Y, Pvt.room:Y, Locker:N, Recep:ltd; Note: laundry, billiards, safe deposit, c.c., central, miners allowed, YHA

Kalgoorlie Backpackers, 166 Hay Street, Kalgoorlie WA; T:0890911482, *info@ kalgoorliebackpackers.com.au/*; $34bed, Kitchen:N, B'fast:N, WiFi:Y, Pvt. room:Y, Locker:N, Recep:24/7; Note: parking, wh/chair ok, laundry, pool, billiards, luggage rm, c.c. ok

MARGARET RIVER is a town in extreme southwestern Australia, situated some 170mi/270km south of Perth. Once home to timber and agriculture, wine and tourism are more important today. There are caves, dolphins, whales, and surfing, too.

www.margaretriver.com/

Surfpoint@Prevelly B'packers, 12 Riedle Dr, Gnarabup, Margaret River WA; T:(08)97571777, *office@ surfpoint.com.au/*; $31bed, Kitchen:Y, B'fast:N, WiFi:Y, Pvt.room:N, Locker:N, Recep:ltd; Note: parking, .wh/chair ok, laundry, pool, billiards, luggage rm, beach

PERTH had been inhabited by the Whadjuk Noongar people for over 40,000 years before being sighted by Europeans in 1697. That made it the first, though it was last to actually join the federation in 1901, having been founded as a city in 1829. Today it is the other city of Australia, number four, situated on the far west coast far removed from its big brothers back east and, at almost two million souls, far bigger than anything else on its own shore. It is the capital of Western Australia, of course, and claimed its stake in the future through a series of gold rushes in the 19th century. It demanded a railway be built to connect it to the rest of the country before joining the federation. Today it is a modern multicultural city, complete with museums and festivals, and closer to some foreign capitals than to its own capital back east.

www.experienceperth.com/

Beatty Lodge, 235 Vincent St, West Perth, WA; T:+61/892271521, *info@ beattylodge.com.au/*; $36bed, Kitchen:Y, B'fast:N, WiFi:Y, Pvt.room:Y, Locker:N, Recep:ltd; Note: billiards, tour desk, pool, c.c. ok, laundry, parking, free bus>town

The Emperor's Crown Backpackers, 85 Stirling St, Perth WA; T:0892271400, *info@ emperorscrown.com.au/*; $34bed, Kitchen:Y, B'fast:N, WiFi:Y, Pvt.room:Y, Locker:N, Recep:ltd; Note: tour desk, wh/chair ok, laundry, parking, luggage room, central

Ocean Beach B'packers, cnr Marine Parade/Eric St, Cottesloe Beach; *oceanbeachbackpackers.com/*, T:**0893845111,** *backpackers@obh.com.au;* $30bed,

Kitchen:Y, B'fast:N, WiFi:Y, Pvt.room:Y, Locker:Y, Recep:24/7; Note: resto/bar, parking, tour desk, laundry, luggage room, bikes, loud

Witch's Hat Backpackers, 148 Palmerston St, Perth WA; T:(08)92284228, *manager@ witchs-hat.com/*; $35bed, Kitchen:Y, B'fast:N, WiFi:Y, Pvt.room:Y, Locker:Y, Recep:24/7; Note: parking, tour desk, laundry, luggage room, ac, c.c. ok, not central

Underground Backpackers, 268 Newcastle St, Northbridge WA; *undergroundbackpackers.com.au/*, T:(08)92283755, *underground@iinet.net.au*; $30bed, Kitchen:Y, B'fast:Y, WiFi:Y, Pvt.room:Y, Locker:N, Recep:24/7; Note: bar, laundry, pool, central

Britannia on William, 253 William St, Northbridge WA; *perthbritannia. com/*, T:(08)92276000; $31bed, Kitchen:Y, B'fast:N, WiFi:Y, Pvt.room:Y, Locker:N, Recep:24/7; Note: laundry, c.c. ok, big, central

Hay Street Backpackers, 266 Hay St, East Perth WA; *haystbackpackers. com/*, T:(08)92219880, *haystbackpackers@gmail.com*; $36bed, Kitchen:Y, B'fast:N, WiFi:Y, Pvt.room:Y, Locker:N, Recep:ltd; Note: tour desk, laundry, c.c. ok, pool, a/c, close to town

Coolibah Lodge, 194 Brisbane St, Northbridge WA; *coolibahlodge.com.au/*, T:(08)93289958; $33bed, Kitchen:Y, B'fast:Y, WiFi:$, Pvt.room:Y, Locker:N, Recep:24/7; Note: bar, billiards, tour desk, laundry, c.c. ok, a/c, central

1201 East Backpackers, 195 Hay St, East Perth WA; TF:1800001201, *info@ 1201east.com.au/*; $33bed, Kitchen:Y, B'fast:Y, WiFi:$, Pvt.room:Y, Locker:N, Recep:ltd; Note: bar, billiards, tour desk, laundry, c.c. ok, a/c, luggage room, CBD

Western Beach Lodge, 6 Westborough St, Scarborough WA; *westernbeach. com/*, T:(08)92451624, *westernbeach@iprimus.com.au*; $33bed, Kitchen:Y, B'fast:N, WiFi:Y, Pvt.room:Y, Locker:Y, Recep:>9p; Note: parking, laundry, luggage room, near beach far from city, long-stays

Exclusive Backpackers, 156 Adelaide Terrace, East Perth WA; *exclusivebackpackers.com/*, T:0892219991; *exclusivebackpackers@hotmail.com*;

$31bed, Kitchen:Y, B'fast:N, WiFi:Y, Pvt.room:Y, Locker:N, Recep:>10p; Note: min stay 2N, resto, parking, tour desk, laundry, safe deposit, c.c. ok

The Shiralee Backpackers Hostel, 107 Brisbane St, Perth, WA; T:0892277448, *info@ shiralee.com.au/*; $27bed, Kitchen:Y, B'fast:Y, WiFi:Y, Pvt. room:Y, Locker:N, Desk hr:ltd; Note: bar, tour desk, laundry, c.c. ok, a/c, luggage room, long-stays, basic

Globe Backpackers, 561 Wellington St, Perth WA; *globebackpackers.com. au/*, T:(08)93214080, *globebak@iinet.net.au*; $29bed, Kitchen:Y, B'fast:N, WiFi:Y, Pvt.room:Y, Locker:Y, Recep:24/7; Note: billiards, tour desk, laundry, pool, central, wh/chair ok, near trans

WALPOLE is a town of a few hundred 260mi/420km south of Perth on the most southwestern tip of Australia. The Bibbulmun Track—a 600mi/1000km hiking path through the outback—passes through it.
www.westernaustralia.com/en/Destination/Walpole/9027929

Walpole Lodge, Park Ave, Walpole WA; T:0898401244, *info@ walpolelodge. com.au/*; $27bed, Kitchen:Y, B'fast:N, WiFi:Y, Pvt.room:Y, Locker:N, Recep:ltd; Note: wh/chair ok, luggage rm, billiards, c.c. ok, parking, laundry, parking

Part II: New Zealand

New Zealand is to Australia as Canada is to the US, more or less, the little brother by default, whether they like it or not, when in fact their histories are entirely separate. Surprising to most, NZ is actually quite isolated (ha! pun: island=*isola*), some 900mi/1500km to the east of Australia, and almost as far south of Fiji. The Polynesian Maori only got here around 1250-1300, a few short centuries before the Europeans in 1642. They found *moa* birds, 12ft/3.6mt tall and 500lb/225kg in weight, and proceeded to eat them to extinction, KFC wrappers and empty ketchup bottles littering ancient middens, just jokinggggg... What Europeans later found was a complete island culture adapted toward much cooler climes, the largest city Auckland — on the north island — at the same latitude as mainland Australia's most southerly (coolest) city Melbourne, or as far south as San Francisco, US, is north, i.e. chilly sometimes. The southern island can be downright arctic — I mean 'antarctic' — with glaciers and all, only South America's Tierra del Fuego farther south on this blue planet.

After thirty-five years of "Musket Wars" between rival tribes, New Zealand became a colony of the British Empire in 1840. There then followed the "New Zealand Wars," also called the "Maori Land Wars." You can guess the rest; Maoris lost most of their land. Since then, New Zealand has largely followed the pattern of a modern liberal democracy, with a welfare state and progressive politics, especially with respect to the environment. Though generally in step with big brother Australia, with which it shares immigrants and open borders, in some ways it's even more progressive, as in relations with its neighboring Pacific countries and its own minority groups. If wool used to be almost the only business and product for export, then today that's no longer the case, and the economy has diversified recently in many directions, tourism not the least of them.

If the main tourist draw is the natural countryside, then a strong secondary draw is the modern urban culture of the cities. There are also ancient *pa,*

Maori fortified settlements of archeological interest. Musical, artistic, and athletic traditions are strong. Hippie lifestyles are legendary. Back when I lived in Oregon in the 1980's, the US's "last bastion of the terminally hip," New Zealand was the Promised Land. The Tolkien trilogy was filmed here. People call themselves 'Kiwis,' after the national bird. Hostels here are good, though you're not likely to get free WiFi. More than anywhere else in the world, though, hostels are almost the norm here, and there are all types: high-rise, home-stay, dirt-scuzzy, or fun-and-play. Currency is the New Zealand ('kiwi') dollar (NZD). The languages are English and Maori. Calling code is +64.

www.newzealand.com

9) New Zealand: North Island

The north island is the one that's warm and Polynesian, with beaches and most of the population. But don't worry: only a narrow strait separates the two, and they are both long and narrow. Be prepared for some latitude adjustments.

AUCKLAND is the largest city in New Zealand, with almost a million and a half inhabitants, thirty-one percent of the country's total and the largest Polynesian city in the world. It lies north of most of the northern island, at the point where it starts looking like the South Pacific island that it is. Strung like Christmas lights on isthmuses and bridges, it looks like nothing so much as a wedding cake, or maybe San Francisco. It has harbors on both sides of the island. It was numerous with Maori even before the arrival of Europeans, with as many as 20,000 people in the area. Inter-tribal warfare with the arrival of firearms devastated the local population and put the new city at risk, too, leading to a disproportionate number of ex-soldiers — particularly Irish — being recruited to bolster the garrison in cases of emergency... in return for free passage. The next century was simpler for Auckland, as it proceded along the familiar highway to modernization as practiced by its role models in Australia and the US.

That means multiculturalism, always a sensitive issue. More and more Auckland is less and less white/Anglo and more and more Asian. That's no surprise, since it rates so highly on liveability indices. That means lots of amenities and activities for tourists, too. For culture there are the Auckland Art Gallery, the Auckland War Memorial Museum, the National Maritime Museum, and Museum of Transport and Technology (MOTAT). Auckland scores even

higher for nature. Besides the Auckland Zoo and the Sea Life Aquarium, there are parks like Auckland Domain, one of the largest parks in the city, and smaller ones like Albert Park, Myers Park, Western Park and Victoria Park. Other urban landmarks include the Auckland Civic Theatre, Harbour Bridge, Auckland Town Hall, Aotea Square, and St. Patrick's Cathedral. Other natural attractions include Mount Eden, Mount Victoria, One Tree Hill, Rangitoto Island, and Waiheke Island. Or if you want to be like the locals, then get on a boat.
www.aucklandnz.com/

Ponsonby Backpackers, 2 Franklin Rd, Ponsonby, Auckland, NZ; T:093601311, *info@ ponsonby-backpackers.co.nz/*; $22bed, Kitchen:Y, B'fast:N, WiFi:Y, Pvt.room:Y, Locker:Y, Recep:ltd, Note: bikes, tour desk, laundry, parking, c.c. ok, luggage rm, not central

Surf n'Snow Backpackers, 102 Albert St, Auckland, NZ; T:+64(09)3638889, *info@ surfandsnow.co.nz/*; $19bed, Kitchen:Y, B'fast:N, WiFi:Y, Pvt.room:Y, Locker:Y, Recep:24/7; Note: central, tour desk, wheelchair ok, c.c. ok, laundry

Nomads Fat Camel, 38 Fort St, Downtown, Auckland, T:0508NOMADS;

Nomads Auckland, 16 - 20 Fort St, Auckland, NZ; T:0508666237, *bookings@ nomadsworld.com/*; $19bed, Kitchen:Y, B'fast:N, WiFi:$, Pvt.room:Y, Locker:Y, Recep:24/7; Note: central, resto/bar, club, lift, wh/chair ok, free tour/info, sauna, c.c. ok

Silverfern Backpackers, 234 Hobson St, Auckland, NZ; T:093779604, *info@ silverfernbackpackers.co.nz/*; $16bed, Kitchen:Y, B'fast:Y, WiFi:Y, Pvt. room:Y, Locker:N, Recep:ltd; Note: free tour/info, wheelchair ok, parking, c.c. ok, central, warm

BASE Auckland, Level 3, 229 Queen St, Auckland, NZ; T:+64(09)3584877, *auckland@ stayatbase.com/*; $17bed, Kitchen:Y, B'fast:N, WiFi:$, Pvt.room:Y, Locker:Y, Recep:24/7; Note: bar, free tour/info, games, laundry, a/c, central

K Road City Travelers, 146 Karangahape Rd, Auckland, NZ; T:093099474, *admin@ kroadcitytravelers.co.nz/*; $25bed, Kitchen:Y, B'fast:Y, WiFi:Y, Pvt. room:Y, Locker:Y, Recep:>11p; Note: nr Airbus stop, laundry, c.c. ok, central

9) New Zealand: North Island

YHA Auckland, 20 Liverpool St, Auckland, NZ; T:+64(0)93092802, *yhaauck@ yha.co.nz/;* $17bed, Kitchen:Y, B'fast:N, WiFi:$, Pvt.room:Y, Locker:N, Recep:24/7; Note: free tour/info, lift, ATM, c.c. ok, central, nr Airbus, member disc

Freemans Lodge, 65 Wellington St, Freemans Bay, Auckland, NZ; *freemansbackpackers.co.nz/,* T:093765046, *freemansbb@xtra.co.nz;* $27bed, Kitchen:Y, B'fast:$, WiFi:Y, Pvt.room:Y, Locker:Y, Recep:ltd; Note: resto, parking, tour desk, laundry, c.c. ok, coffee/tea, central

City Garden Lodge, 25 St Georges Bay Rd, Parnell, Auckland NZ; *citygardenlodge.co.nz/,* T:093020880, *city.garden@compuweb.co.nz;* $23bed, Kitchen:Y, B'fast:N, WiFi:Y, Pvt.room:Y, Locker:N, Recep:ltd; Note: free tour/ info, laundry, luggage rm, parking, c.c. ok

Frienz.com Backpackers, 27/31 Victoria St. E, Auckland, NZ; T:+64(09)3076437, *auck@ frienz.com/;* $19bed, Kitchen:Y, B'fast:N, WiFi:Y, Pvt. room:Y, Locker:Y, Recep:ltd; Note: lift, free tour/info, luggage rm, laundry, c.c. ok

Airport Skyway Lodge, 30 Kirkbride Rd, Mangere, Auckland NZ; T:+64(09)2754443, *e-mail@ skywaylodge.co.nz/;* $32bed, Kitchen:Y, B'fast:N, WiFi:Y, Pvt.room:Y, Locker:N, Recep:24/7; Note: parking, luggage room, laundry

Oaklands Lodge, 5A Oaklands Rd, Mt Eden, Auckland, NZ; T:+64(09)6386545, *info@ oaklands.co.nz/;* $19bed, Kitchen:Y, B'fast:N, WiFi:Y, Pvt.room:Y, Locker:Y, Recep:ltd, Note: free tour, info, laundry, luggage rm, parking, c.c. ok, not central

BK Hostel, 3 Mercury Lane, Auckland Central, NZ; *bkhostel.co.nz/,* T:+64(09)3070052, *bkhostel@joy.net.nz;* $24bed, Kitchen:Y, B'fast:N, WiFi:Y, Pvt. room:Y, Locker:N, Recep:ltd; Note: tour desk, luggage room, laundry, c.c. ok, nr Airbus

Lantana Lodge, 60 St Georges Bay Rd, Parnell, Auckland, NZ; *lantanalodge. co.nz/,* T:+64/93734546, *lantanalodge@xtra.co.nz;* $22bed, Kitchen:Y, B'fast:N,

WiFi:Y, Pvt.room:Y, Locker:N, Recep:ltd; Note: tour desk, laundry, c.c. ok, central, hilly 'hood

City Travellers Auckland, 93 Anzac Ave, Auckland, NZ; T:0508737378, *citytravellersauckland.blackstone.co.nz/*,; $19bed, Kitchen:Y, B'fast:N, WiFi:Y, Pvt.room:Y, Locker:N, Recep:7a-10p; Note: central, laundry, c.c. ok

COROMANDEL is a town on the peninsula of the same name only 45mi/75km from Auckland as the crow flies, 120mi/190km by road, and home to almost 1500. Once a scene of gold rushes, its specialty now is tourism, that and arts and crafts and hippies and... pulling mussels from shells.
www.thecoromandel.com/

Anchor Lodge, 448 Wharf Rd, Coromandel Town, NZ; T:078667992, *info@ anchorlodgecoromandel.co.nz/*; $22bed, Kitchen:Y, B'fast:N, WiFi:Y, Pvt.room:Y, Locker:N, Recep:ltd; Note: pool, parking, tour desk, laundry, luggage rm, wh/chair ok

GREAT BARRIER ISLAND is one of the largest of New Zealand's lesser islands at 110sq.mi/285sq.km, and lies some 62mi/100km northeast of Auckland. It is inhabited by almost a thousand people and the main industries are farming and tourism. The main attraction is to witness the old-fashioned side of New Zealand, the only electricity your own. It's rustic. Mail was once delivered by pigeon.
www.thebarrier.co.nz/

Stray Possum Lodge, Cape Barrier Rd, Great Barrier Island, NZ; T:+64(09)4290109, *info@ straypossum.co.nz/*; $19bed, Kitchen:Y, B'fast:N, WiFi:N, Pvt.room:Y, Locker:N, Recep:ltd; Note: resto/bar, tour desk, billiards, games, c.c. ok, outback

Neptunes Intl Backpackers, 43 Gresson St, Greymouth, NZ; *awakekiwi. wix.com/neptunes/*, T:037684425, *emailneptunes@gmail.com*; $23bed, Kitchen:Y, B'fast:Y, WiFi:Y, Pvt.room:Y, Locker:N, Recep:ltd; Note: tents ok, bike rent, games, laundry, luggage room, parking

Duke Hostel, 27 Guinness St, Greymouth, NZ; *duke.co.nz/*, T:+64(03)7689470, *dukenz@clear.net.nz*; $24bed, Kitchen:Y, B'fast:Y, WiFi:Y, Pvt.room:Y, Locker:N, Recep:ltd; Note: bar, parking, games, luggage room, laundry, soup, beer

Noah's Ark Backpackers, 16 Chapel St, Greymouth, NZ; T:+64/37684868, *stay@ noahs.co.nz/*; $23bed, Kitchen:Y, B'fast:N, WiFi:Y, Pvt.room:Y, Locker:N, Recep:ltd; Note: hot tub, bike rent, games, laundry, luggage rm, parking, c.c. ok

YHA Greymouth, 15 Alexander St, Greymouth, NZ; T:+64(03)7684951, *yhagymth@ yha.co.nz/*; $24bed, Kitchen:Y, B'fast:N, WiFi:Y, Pvt.room:Y, Locker:N, Recep:8a>8p; Note: parking, tour desk, laundry, wh/chair ok, c.c. ok, quiet, bars

HAMILTON is a center of higher education and one of the fastest-growing areas of New Zealand. With around 200,000 people, it's one of the largest already, only 80mi/130km south of Auckland. The setting on the Waikato River is scenic and the town rocks. Soundscape and Parachute are major music festivals. Then there are the Fringe Festival and the Underground Film Festival, way cool.
www.visithamilton.co.nz/

J's Backpackers, 8 Grey St, Hamilton East, NZ; T:+64(07)856 8934, *admin@ jsbackpackers.co.nz/*, $25bed, Kitchen:Y, B'fast:N, WiFi:Y, Pvt.room:Y, Locker:N, Recep:ltd; Note: laundry, safe dep, c.c. ok, bus stn shuttle

YHA Hamilton, 140 Ulster St, Hamilton, NZ; *yha.co.nz/*, T:+64/79571848; *hamilton@microtel.co.nz;*$21bed, Kitchen:Y, B'fast:N, WiFi:Y, Pvt.room:Y, Locker:N, Recep:ltd; Note: nr ctr/bus, parking, laundry, wh/chair ok, c.c. ok

NAPIER is a city of almost 60,000 on the west coast of the north island. It is a seaport, and with the inland city of Hastings, comprises New Zealand's fifth-largest urban area, with a population of over 120,000. It lies some 190mi/320km north of Wellington, in a major wool and fruit-producing

agricultural area, for which it is the port. Its 1930's Art Deco architecture is the big tourist attraction... that, and the wine. Nightlife's good.
www.napiercity.co.nz/

YHA Napier, 277 Marine Parade, Napier, NZ; T:+64/33195931, *yha. napier@ yha.co.nz/*; $25bed, Kitchen:Y, B'fast:N, WiFi:Y, Pvt.room:Y, Locker:N, Recep:ltd; Note: tour desk, parking, laundry, c.c. ok, nr beach & town

NATIONAL PARK VILLAGE sits at 2400ft/825mt on the border of the World Heritage Tongariro National Park in the center of the north island. With great views of the mountain, tourism is the main industry. That means skiiing in the winter, hiking and biking in the summer. Tranz Scenic's 'The Overlander' train stops here for lunch.
www.nationalpark.co.nz/

Howards Lodge, 11-13 Caroll St, National Park Village, NZ; *howardslodge. co.nz/*, T:+64(07)8922827; $25bed, Kitchen:N, B'fast:$, WiFi:Y, Pvt.room:Y, Locker:N, Recep:ltd; Note: log fires, tour desk, parking, laundry, wh/chair ok, c.c. ok, billiards

Natl Park Hotel/Hostel, 61 Carroll St, National Park Village, NZ; *nationalparkhoteltongariro.co.nz/*, T:078922805, *nationalparkhotel@xtra.co.nz*; $21bed, Kitchen:Y, B'fast:N, WiFi:Y, Pvt.room:Y, Locker:N, Recep:ltd; Note: resto/bar, billiards, tour desk, parking, laundry, luggage rm, c.c. ok

The Park Travellers' Lodge, 2/6 Millar St, National Park, NZ; T:078922748, *bookings@ the-park.co.nz/*; $32bed, Kitchen:Y, B'fast:N, WiFi:Y, Pvt.room:Y, Locker:N, Recep:ltd; Note: resto/bar, tour desk, parking, laundry, luggage rm, c.c. ok

Ski Haus, Cnr Caroll/McKenzie Sts, National Park Village NZ; *skihaus. co.nz/*, T:078922854, *skihaus@xtra.co.nz*; $23bed, Kitchen:Y, B'fast:$, WiFi:Y, Pvt. room:Y, Locker:N, Recep:ltd; Note: billiards, tour desk, laundry, luggage rm, c.c. ok, log fire

YHA National Park Backpackers, 4 Finlay St, National Park Village, NZ; *yha.co.nz/*, T:+6478922870, *nat.park.backpackers@xtra.co.nz*; $22bed, Kitchen:Y,

B'fast:N, WiFi:Y, Pvt.room:Y, Locker:N, Recep:ltd; Note: tour desk, parking, laundry, wh/chair ok, c.c. ok, central

NELSON is an urban area of 60,000 located in the center of the country on the north coast of the south island, on Tasman Bay. It is known for its arts and crafts scene, with festivals such as the Nelson Arts Festival and Wearable Art Awards. For music there are the Nelson School of Music's Winter Music Festival, the Adam New Zealand Festival of Chamber Music, and the annual Nelson Jazz Festival.
www.nelson.nz.com/

Tasman Bay Backpackers, 10 Weka St, Nelson, NZ; T:+64(03)5487950, *stay@ tasmanbaybackpackers.co.nz/*; $22bed, Kitchen:Y, B'fast:N, WiFi:Y, Pvt. room:Y, Locker:N, Recep:ltd; Note: bike rent, tour desk, laundry, luggage room, c.c. ok, parking

YHA Nelson, 59 Rutherford St, Nelson, NZ; T:+64/35459988, *yhanels@ yha. co.nz/*; $25bed, Kitchen:Y, B'fast:N, WiFi:Y, Pvt.room:Y, Locker:$, Recep:8a>8p; Note: arpt shuttle, laundry, luggage room, c.c. ok, games, central

Accents on the Park, 335 Trafalgar Square, Nelson, NZ; *accentsonthepark.com/*, T:+64(03)5484335; $21bed, Kitchen:Y, B'fast:N, WiFi:Y, Pvt.room:N, Locker:N, Recep:24/7; Note: bar, parking, tour desk, laundry, luggage room, wh/chair ok

Paradiso Backpackers Hostel, 42 Weka St, Nelson; *backpackernelson.co.nz/*, T:0800269667; $19bed, Kitchen:Y, B'fast:Y, WiFi:Y, Pvt.room:Y, Locker:Y, Recep:ltd; Note: pool, sauna, tour desk, soup, luggage rm, party, wh/chair ok

Custom House, 252 Haven Rd, Stepneyville, Nelson, NZ; *customhousenelson. co.nz/*, T:+64(03)5458365; $22bed, Kitchen:Y, B'fast:N, WiFi:Y, Pvt.room:Y, Locker:N, Recep:ltd; Note: bar, billiards, parking, laundry, luggage room, bikes, not central

NEW PLYMOUTH sits on the west coast of the north island, and is the largest city of the Taranaki region, with a population over 50,000. The city has dairy

and petroleum industries, in addition to tourism. Mountains and coast are both accessible. Outdoor sports are popular.
www.newplymouthnz.com/Events/

Ariki Backpackers, 25 Ariki St, Taranaki 4342, NZ; T:+64(06)7695020, *stay@ arikibackpackers.com/*; $25bed, Kitchen:Y, B'fast:Y, WiFi:Y, Pvt.room:Y, Locker:N, Recep:ltd; Note: central, resto/bar, free tour/info, luggage room, laundry, c.c. ok

Egmont Eco Lodge YHA, 12 Clawton St, Westown, New Plymouth, NZ; T:+64/67535720, *yha.kaikoura@ yha.co.nz/*; $24bed, Kitchen:Y, B'fast:N, WiFi:Y, Pvt.room:Y, Locker:N, Recep:ltd; Note: tour desk, parking, laundry, c.c. ok, safe dep

PAIHIA is the main tourist town on the Bay of Islands 35mi/60km north of Whangerai on the north island. It was first settled in 1823 and is now home to almost two thousand people. It is close to the historic town of Russell and Haruru Falls.
www.paihia.co.nz

Base Bay of Islands, 18 Kings Road, Paihia, Bay of Islands NZ; T:+64/94027111, *bayofislands@ stayatbase.com/*; $23bed, Kitchen:Y, B'fast:N, WiFi:$, Pvt.room:N, Locker:$, Recep:ltd; Note: pool, bar, parking, tour desk, laundry, luggage rm, wh/chair ok

Saltwater Lodge, 14 Kings Road, Paihia, NZ; *saltwaterlodge.co.nz/*, T:+64(09)4027075, $22bed, Kitchen:Y, B'fast:N, WiFi:$, Pvt.room:Y, Locker:N, Recep:ltd; Note: bikes beach bbq, parking, tour desk, laundry, luggage rm, c.c. ok

YHA Paihia, Corner King's/McMurray Rd, Paihia, NZ; T:+64/94027487, *yha.paihia@ yha.co.nz/*; $23bed, Kitchen:Y, B'fast:N, WiFi:$, Pvt.room:Y, Locker:$, Recep:ltd; Note: parking, tour desk, laundry, luggage rm, c.c. ok, nr beach, quiet

Bay Adventure, 28 Kings Road, Paihia, NZ; T:+64/94025163, *info@ bayadventurer.co.nz/*; $22bed, Kitchen:Y, B'fast:$, WiFi:$, Pvt.room:Y, Locker:Y,

Recep:ltd; Note: pool, parking, tour desk, laundry, luggage rm, c.c. ok, hot tub, bikes

ROTORUA is a city of 68,700 located 140mi/230km southeast of Auckland. It is a tourist town known for its geothermal activity – geysers, hot springs, and hot mud pools. There is also a Buried Village, victim of the 1886 Mount Tarawera eruption. In addition there are many lakes surrounding the city. It it known as 'Sulphur City.' You can guess the rest. There are also botanic gardens and historic architecture.

www.rotoruanz.com/

Astray Motel & Backpackers, 1202 Pukuatua St, Rotorua, NZ; T:(07)3481200, *reservations@ astray.co.nz/*; $20bed, Kitchen:Y, B'fast:N, WiFi:Y, Pvt.room:Y, Locker:N, Recep:>9p; Note: tour desk, wh/chair ok, parking, a/c, c.c. ok, central, nr bus, cozy

Rotorua Planet Backpackers, 1080 Eruera St, Rotorua, T:073502550; *rotoruaplanetbackpackers@xtra.co.nz*; $21bed, Kitchen:Y, B'fast:Y, Pvt.room:Y, *rotoruaplanetbackpackers.co.nz/*, Locker:Y, Recep:24/7; Note: central, tour desk, laundry, luggage room, parking, c.c. ok, nr bus

Base Rotorua, 1286 Arawa St, Rotorua, NZ; T:+64/73488636, *rotorua@ stayatbase.com/*; $22bed, Kitchen:Y, B'fast:$, WiFi:Y, Pvt.room:Y, Locker:Y, Recep:24/7; Note: geo-thermal, real beds, Maori culture, bar, tour desk, laundry

Crash Palace, 1271 Hinemaru St, Rotorua, NZ; T:08008927274, *info@ crashpalace.co.nz/*; $18bed, Kitchen:Y, B'fast:$, WiFi:Y, Pvt.room:Y, Locker:N, Recep:8a-9p; Note: bar, pool, parking, wheelchair ok, free food, luggage room, games

Spa Lodge, 1221 Amohau St, Rotorua, NZ; T:+64(07)3483486, *info@ spalodge.co.nz/*; $19bed, Kitchen:Y, B'fast:N, WiFi:Y, Pvt.room:Y, Locker:N, Recep:>10p; Note: central, tour desk, laundry, luggage room, parking, c.c. ok

Cactus Jack Backpackers, 1210 Haupapa St, Rotorua, NZ; *cactusjackbackpackers.co.nz/*, T:0800122228, *cactusjackbp@xtra.co.nz*; $16bed,

Kitchen:Y, B'fast:N, WiFi:$, Pvt.room:Y, Locker:N, Recep:ltd; Note: hot tub, bike rent, billiards, tour desk, laundry, c.c. ok, basic

TAIRUA is a town of over 1200 inhabitants on the east side of the Coromandel Peninsula on the north island. With an economy originally built on gold mining and timber, it is now a tourist town, with water-based activities predominant.
www.tairua.org.nz

Tairua Beach House, 342A Main Rd, Tairua, NZ; *tairuabeachhouse.co.nz/*, T:+64(07)8648313; $19bed, Kitchen:Y, B'fast:N, WiFi:Y, Pvt.room:Y, Locker:Y, Recep:24/7; Note: tour desk, laundry, c.c. ok

TAUPO is a tourist town in the center of the north island on the shores of Lake Taupo. It is a scene of geothermal activity, with several hot springs and nearby volcano Mt. Tauhara. There are forests and waterfalls in the area. There are also sky diving, jet boating and paragliding available.

www.greatlaketaupo.com

Base Taupo, 7 Tuwharetoa St, Taupo Town Centre, NZ; T:+64(07)3774464, *taupo@ stayatbase.com/*; $24bed, Kitchen:Y, B'fast:N, WiFi:Y, Pvt.room:Y, Locker:N, Recep:24/7; Note: bar/club, tour desk, wheelchair ok, laundry, luggage $, club noise

Tiki Lodge, 104 Tuwharetoa St, Taupo, NZ; T:+6473774545, *stayat@ tikilodge. co.nz/*; $23bed, Kitchen:Y, B'fast:N, WiFi:Y, Pvt.room:Y, Locker:N, Recep:>8p; Note: wheelchair ok, tour desk, luggage room, laundry, parking, c.c. ok

Taupo Urban Retreat, Heuheu St, Taupo, NZ; T:0800872261, *stay@ tur. co.nz/*; $21bed, Kitchen:Y, B'fast:N, WiFi:Y, Pvt.room:Y, Locker:Y, Recep:ltd; Note: bar, w/chair ok, tour desk, luggage rm, laundry, parking

Berkenhoff Lodge, 75 Scannell St, Taupo, NZ; *berkenhofflodge.co.nz/*, T:+64(07)3784909, *bhoff@reap.org.nz*; $21bed, Kitchen:Y, B'fast:N, WiFi:Y, Pvt. room:Y, Locker:N, Recep:ltd; Note: resto/bar, parking, pool, laundry, not central, tour desk, games

Bradshaws Lodge, 130 Heuheu St, Taupo Town Centre, NZ; T:073788288, *info@ bradshawslodge.com/*; $29bed, Kitchen:Y, B'fast:Y, WiFi:Y, Pvt.room:Y, Locker:N, Recep:ltd; Note: tour desk, laundry, luggage room, c.c. ok, not central

Rainbow Lodge, 99 Titiraupenga St, Taupo, NZ; *rainbowlodge.co.nz/*, T:+6473785754; $20bed, Kitchen:Y, B'fast:N, WiFi:Y, Pvt.room:Y, Locker:N, Recep:ltd; Note: wh/chair ok, tour desk, parking, luggage room, laundry, a/c

TAURANGA is the largest city on the northern Bay of Plenty on the north island. It has a population over 120,000. It is one of New Zealand's fastest-growing cities; its northerly warm climate makes it prime agricultural acreage. It is also popular with divers and swimmers.

www.newzealand.com/int/tauranga

YHA Tauranga, 171 Elizabeth St, Tauranga, NZ; T:+64/75785064, *yhataur@ yha.co.nz/*; $21bed, Kitchen:Y, B'fast:N, WiFi:Y, Pvt.room:Y, Locker:Y, Recep:8a>7p; Note: tour desk, parking, laundry, wh/chair ok, c.c. ok, far, YHA disc.

Harbourside City Backpackers, 105 The Strand, Tauranga, NZ; T:075794066, *info@ backpacktauranga.co.nz/*; $24bed, Kitchen:Y, B'fast:N, WiFi:Y, Pvt.room:Y, Locker:N, Recep:>9p; Note: aquatic activities, tour desk, laundry, c.c. ok, safe dep, bikes, central

THAMES is a town of almost 7000 on the west side of the Coromandel Peninsula on the north island. During its gold rush, it was the second largest city in New Zealand. The town still has a historic district.

www.thamesinfo.co.nz/home

Sunkist International Backpackers, 506 Brown St, Thames, NZ; T:078688808, *info@ sunkistbackpackers.com/*; $19bed, Kitchen:Y, B'fast:Y, WiFi:Y, Pvt.room:Y, Locker:Y, Recep:ltd; Note: tour desk, parking, laundry, c.c. ok, billiards, safe dep, TV, dog

TWIZEL is a town of one thousand people in the Mackenzie Basin of the south island. Originally intended as a temporary town to build the Upper Waitaki Hydroelectricity Scheme, the town peaked at 6000 residents in the 1970's and successfully sued to save itself. Today it serves as a tourist town with access to Lake Ruataniwha for summer activities and to Ohau Skifield and the Round Hill Ski Area in winter.

www.twizelnz.com

High Country Lodge/Backpackers, 23 Mackenzie Dr, Twizel, NZ; T:+64/34350671, *info@ highcountrylodge.co.nz/*; $21bed, Kitchen:Y, B'fast:N, WiFi:Y, Pvt.room:Y, Locker:N, Recep:ltd; Note: tour desk, parking, laundry, wh/chair ok, c.c., luggage rm, central

WAITOMO CAVES are a tourist attraction in the northern part of the northern island. This includes leading hundreds of tourists through the limestone landscape, stalactites, stalagmites and glowworm caves, and leading tiny groups into tiny holes and networks.

www.waitomo.com

Kiwi Paka, Hotel Access Road, Waitomo Caves, NZ; *waitomo.kiwipaka. co.nz/*, T:078783395, *waitomobackpackders@xtra.co.nz*; $27bed, Kitchen:Y, B'fast:N, WiFi:Y, Pvt.room:Y, Locker:N, Recep:ltd; Note: resto/bar, parking, laundry, wh/chair ok, c.c. ok, luggage rm, games

Juno Hall YHA Waitomo, 600 Waitomo Caves Rd., Waitomo Caves, NZ; *yha.co.nz/*, T:+64/78787649, *junowaitomo@xtra.co.nz*; $25bed, Kitchen:Y, B'fast:N, WiFi:Y, Pvt.room:Y, Locker:N, Recep:7a>8p; Note: tents ok, pool, tour desk, parking, laundry, c.c. ok, no shops, far

WANGANUI, is also spelled with a "wh" and is located on the west coast of the lower north island, 120mi/200km north of Wellington. The area has always been sacred to and contested by the Maori, and the history is replete with conspiracies and scandals. Tourism is beginning to play an increasing role in the economy.

www.wanganui.com/

Anndion Lodge, 143 Anzac Parade, Wanganui, NZ; T:+64/63433593, *info@ anndionlodge.co.nz/*; $29bed, Kitchen:Y, B'fast:$, WiFi:Y, Pvt.room:Y, Locker:N, Recep:ltd; Note: arpt pickup, pool, bar, parking, laundry, wh/chair ok, c.c. ok

Braemar House, 2 Plymouth St, Wanganui, NZ; *yha.co.nz/*; T:+64/63482301, *contact@braemarhouse.co.nz*; $23bed, Kitchen:Y, B'fast:N, WiFi:Y, Pvt.room:Y, Locker:N, Recep:8a>8p; Note: arpt pickup, tour desk, parking, laundry, nr river/town, safe dep, a/c

WELLINGTON, perched on the southernmost tip of the north island, is the capital of New Zealand, and, with almost 400,000, is its second (or third) largest city, depending on how you count, I guess. It took over as capital from Auckland in 1865, apparently to be more central and more accessible to the south island, undergoing a gold rush at the time. With limited space to sprawl, it has a dense CBD and a picturesque harbor. Architectural landmarks include the Majestic Centre, the State Insurance Building, Futuna Chapel, St. Mary of the Angels, the Bond Store, Town Hall, the Michael Fowler Centre, Wellington Central Library, Capital E, the City-to-Sea Bridge, and the City Gallery. Then there are the government buildings... and the art museums.

Tourism depends heavily on cruise ships and culture, with attractions such as the Museum of Wellington City & Sea, the Wellington Zoo, Zealandia (Karori Wildlife Sanctuary) and Wellington Cable Car. What about festivals, you ask? There are the biennial New Zealand International Arts Festival, biennial Wellington Jazz Festival, biennial Capital E National Arts Festival, the Cuba Street Carnival, New Zealand Fringe Festival, Summer City, The Wellington Folk Festival, Out in the Square, Vodafone Homegrown, the Couch Soup theatre festival, and many film festivals. There is a lively music scene, and an active café culture. Any more questions? There are ferries to cross Cook Strait to the south island.

www.wellingtonnz.com/

Trek Global, 9 O'reily Ave, Wellington, NZ; T:+64(04)4713480, *book@ trekglobal.net/*; $18bed, Kitchen:Y, B'fast:$, WiFi:Y, Pvt.room:Y, Locker:Y, Recep:ltd; Note: free tour/info, lift, bike rent, long-stays, laundry, parking, c.c. ok

Moana Lodge, 49 Moana Rd, Plimmerton, NZ; *moanalodge.co.nz/,* T:+64(04)2332010, *moanalodge@xtra.co.nz*; $31bed, Kitchen:Y, B'fast:N, WiFi:Y,

Pvt.room:Y, Locker:N, Recep:8a>8p; Note: wheelchair ok, tour desk, beach, luggage room, parking, c.c. ok

Downtown Backpackers, 1 Bunny St, Pipitea, Wellington, NZ; T:044738482, *db@ downtownbackpackers.co.nz/*; $24bed, Kitchen:Y, B'fast:$, WiFi:Y, Pvt.room:Y, Locker:$, Recep:24/7; Note: resto/bar, tour desk, laundry, billiards, c.c. ok, central, nr train/ferry

YHA Wellington City, 292 Wakefield St, Wellington, NZ; T:+64/48017280, *yha.wellington@ yha.co.nz/*;$18bed, Kitchen:Y, B'fast:$, WiFi:Y, Pvt. room:Y, Locker:$, Recep:ltd; Note: tour desk, laundry, billiards, c.c. ok, nr supermkt, central

WHANGAREI (pronounced 'Fangarei') is a coastal city in the far north of the northern island, with over 50,000 inhabitants. Mostly an urban center, tourist sites include the volcano Mt. Parihaka, the Hātea River with its waterfall, and Matakoe, or Limestone Island. This is the best shopping in the northland.
www.whangareinz.com

Whangarei Falls Backpackers, 12 Ngunguru Rd, Whangarei, NZ; *whangareifalls.co.nz/*, T:+64(09)4370609; $21bed, Kitchen:Y, B'fast:N, WiFi:Y, Pvt.room:Y, Locker:N, Recep:ltd; Note: tent ok, pool/spa, tour desk, prkng, laundry, c.c. ok, bus pickup

10) South Island

The division between north and south New Zealand reflects geographical realities that almost exactly mirror its sister country Chile halfway around the globe (over the pole is faster; and yes, they fly that route). Up north is warm, almost tropical. Down south is cool, almost Antarctic. The north is Polynesian. The south is Scottish. The north has beaches. The south has glaciers. What else? You can easily do it all in one trip.

AKAROA is a village of less than a thousand people on the south island, whose population can rise up to 15,000 in the summer. Attractions are nature and the romantic British and French colonial history and architecture. It lies 45mi/75km from Christchurch.
www.akaroa.com/

Bon Accord Backpackers, 57 Rue Lavaud, Akaroa, NZ; *bon-accord.co.nz/*, T:+64(03)3047782; $23bed, Kitchen:Y, B'fast:N, WiFi:Y, Pvt.room:Y, Locker:Y, Recep:ltd; Note: parking, tour desk, laundry, luggage rm, c.c. ok

ARTHUR'S PASS is a town in the South Island's Southern Alps that sits 3mi/5km south of the mountain pass of the same name and serves to facilitate access to the eponymous national park. The population is pushing five dozen, plus you. The TranzAlpine Express passes through, considered one of the world's great train journeys for its scenery.
www.arthurspass.com/

Mountain House, P.O. Box 12, Arthur's Pass, NZ; *trampers. co.nz/*, T:033189258; $26bed, Kitchen:Y, B'fast:N, WiFi:Y, Pvt.room:Y, Locker:Y, Recep:ltd; Note: wheelchairs ok, parking, laundry, c.c. ok, shuttle, quiet

CHRISTCHURCH is New Zealand's third-largest city, and is located almost halfway down the south island's east coast. It has over 380,000 inhabitants. Its size and southerly location have made it convenient for Antarctic exploration. It is most famous for the earthquakes that have devastated it twice in the last few years. I can't say much about architecture and landmarks, since so much of it has been destroyed. It is rebuilding along unique designs, with ambitious plans for the future, fashioning itself as "the garden city."
www.christchurch.org.nz/

Point Break Backpackers, 6 Union St, New Brighton, Christchurch, NZ; T:033882050, *mail@ pointbreakbackpackers.co.nz/*; $23bed, Kitchen:Y, B'fast:Y, WiFi:Y, Pvt.room:Y, Locker:Y, Recep:8a>10p; Note: bike rent, luggage room, laundry, parking, c.c. ok, at beach, surfers

Jailhouse Accommodation, 338 Lincoln Rd, Addington, Christchurch, NZ; T:+64(03)9827777, *stay@ jail.co.nz/*; $25bed, Kitchen:Y, B'fast:N, WiFi:$, Pvt.room:Y, Locker:Y, Recep:ltd; Note: tour desk, old prison, laundry, parking, c.c. ok, not central

Kiwi Basecamp, 69 Bealey Ave, Christchurch Central, NZ; T:+64/33666770, *stay@ kiwibasecamp.co.nz/*; $24bed, Kitchen:Y, B'fast:Y, WiFi:$, Pvt.room:Y, Locker:N, Recep:ltd; Note: arpt shuttle, tour desk, wh/chair ok, laundry, nr bus, parking, c.c. ok

Dorset House Backpackers, 1 Dorset St, Christchurch Central. NZ; T:+64(03)3668268, *stay@ dorset.co.nz/*;$30bed, Kitchen:Y, B'fast:N, WiFi:Y, Pvt. room:Y, Locker:N, Recep:ltd; Note: tour desk, luggage rm, laundry, parking, c.c. ok, games

Haka Lodge, 518 Linwood Ave, Woolston, Christchurch, NZ; T:+64(03)9804252, *info@ hakalodge.com/*; $23bed, Kitchen:Y, B'fast:N, WiFi:Y, Pvt.room:Y, Locker:Y, Recep:ltd; Note: tour desk, luggage room, laundry, parking, c.c. ok, a/c, w-chair ok

Canterbury House Backpackers, 257 Bealey Ave, Christchurch; T:033778108, *stay@ canterburyhousebackpackers.co.nz/*, $25bed, Kitchen:Y, B'fast:N, WiFi:Y, Pvt.room:Y, Locker:N, Recep:ltd; Note: tour desk, luggage room, laundry, parking, cats

DUNEDIN is the second-largest city on the south island and largest of the Otago region. Historically significant, it had New Zealand's first university in 1869 and New Zealand's largest population until 1900. Its colonial roots are Scottish. The first settlers came for whales and seals until the Gold Rush of 1861. Meanwhile the Free Church of Scotland founded Dunedin on the model of Edinburgh, with its Gaelic name even. Initial rushes fade, of course, but the

romance remains, and the university provides a constant source of inspiration and initiative. History is ubiquitous here and the arts and music are lively.
www.visit-dunedin.co.nz/

Penny's Backpackers, 6 Stafford St, Dunedin, NZ; T:+64(03)4776027, *info@ pennys.co.nz/*; $22bed, Kitchen:Y, B'fast:N, WiFi:Y, Pvt.room:N, Locker:N, Recep:ltd; Note: bikes, parking, tour desk, laundry, luggage rm, c.c. ok, games

Manor House Backpackers, 28 Manor Place, Dunedin, NZ; T:034770484, *mail@ manorhousebackpackers.co.nz/*; $21bed, Kitchen:Y, B'fast:N, WiFi:Y, Pvt. room:Y, Locker:N, Recep:ltd; Note: central, parking, tour desk, laundry, luggage rm, c.c. ok

Elm Lodge, 74 Elm Row, Dunedin, NZ; *elmlodge.co.nz/*, T:+64(03)4741872, *stay@ elmlodge.co.nz/*; $23bed, Kitchen:Y, B'fast:N, WiFi:Y, Pvt.room:Y, Locker:N, Recep:ltd; Note: parking, laundry, c.c. ok, central

FOX GLACIER, the town of almost 400, serves to accommodate visitors to the glacier itself, one of the most accessible in the world. It is 8mi/13km long and advancing constantly, terminating in rain forest at an elevation of 1000ft/300mt.
www.glaciercountry.co.nz/

Ivory Towers B'packers, 33/35 Sullivan's Rd, S. Westland, Fox Glacier; *ivorytowers.co.nz/*, T:+64/37510838; $23bed, Kitchen:Y, B'fast:N, WiFi:Y, Pvt. room:Y, Locker:N, Recep:ltd; Note: parking, laundry, luggage room, c.c. ok, near ferry, spa

FRANZ JOSEPH (GLACIER) is a small town on the west coast of the south island 3mi/5km from the face of the glacier. The town is surrounded by Westland Tai Poutini National Park. The glacier is currently 7.5mi/12km long and terminates 12mi/19km from the Tasman Sea at an altitude of only 1000ft/300mt above sea level. It has been retreating since 2008. It and its twin Fox Glacier form a UNESCO world heritage site.
www.glaciercountry.co.nz/

Chateau Franz Backpackers, 8/10 Cron St, Franz Josef, NZ; *chateaufranz. co.nz/*, T:+64(03)7520738; $19bed, Kitchen:Y, B'fast:N, WiFi:Y, Pvt.room:Y, Locker:N, Recep:ltd; Note: tour desk, parking, luggage room, laundry, c.c. ok, popcorn

Montrose Lodge, 9 Cron St, Franz Josef, NZ; T:037520188, *reception@ montroselodge.co.nz/*; $18bed, Kitchen:Y, B'fast:N, WiFi:Y, Pvt.room:Y, Locker:N, Recep:ltd; Note: w/chair ok, tour desk, parking, luggage rm, soup, ATM, c.c. ok

YHA Franz Joseph, 24 Cron St, Franz Josef, New Zealand; T:+64(03)7520754, *yhafzjo@ yha.co.nz/*; $18bed, Kitchen:Y, B'fast:N, WiFi:Y, Pvt.room:Y, Locker:N, Recep:8a-8p; Note: nr rain forest, wh/chair ok, tour desk, sauna, luggage rm, laundry

Glow Worm Cottages, 27 Cron St, Franz Josef Glacier, NZ; *glowwormcottages. co.nz/*, T:0800151027; $21bed, Kitchen:Y, B'fast:N, WiFi:Y, Pvt.room:Y, Locker:N, Recep:ltd; Note: w/chair ok, tour desk, parking, laundry, hot tub, free soup

GERALDINE is a town of over two thou 85mi/140km south of Christchurch in the Canterbury region of the South Island. It is known for its history and its arts and crafts. The nearby Peel River has abundant wildlife and birds. The Rangitata River valley was featured in the *Lord of the Rings* trilogy.
www.gogeraldine.co.nz/

Peel Forest Farmstay, 33 Rangitata Gorge Rd, Geraldine, NZ; T:0273050400, *thedeans@ peelforestfarmstay.co/*; $25bed, Kitchen:Y, B'fast:N, WiFi:Y, Pvt. room:Y, Locker:N, Recep:ltd; Note: tour desk, c.c. ok, family-run

HANMER SPRINGS is a small town in the Canterbury region of the South Island, 80mi/130km north of Christchurch. Home to over seven hundred, it is a tourist destination to many more. It is famous for its hot springs, and nature-oriented activities are popular.
www.newzealand.com/int/hanmer-springs/

10) South Island

Hanmer Backpackers, 41 Conical Hill Rd, Hanmer Springs, NZ; T:033157196, *info@ hanmerbackpackers.co.nz/*; $23bed, Kitchen:Y, B'fast:N, WiFi:Y, Pvt.room:Y, Locker:N, Recep:ltd; Note: parking, laundry, wh/chair ok, c.c. ok, luggage room, central

HAVELOCK is a coastal village of almost 500 in the Marlborough region, on the north end of the south island. Once a gold-mining town, it is known for its green mussel trade, its quaint colonial architecture, and its tourism.
www.newzealand.com/us/havelock/

Rutherford YHA, 46 Main Rd, Havelock, NZ; *yha.co.nz/*, T:0800278299, *Bruce2PIES@gmail.com;* $21bed, Kitchen:Y, B'fast:N, WiFi:Y, Pvt.room:Y, Locker:N, Recep:ltd; Note: parking, laundry, tour desk, c.c. ok, safe deposit

HOKITIKA is a town of over 3000 on the west coast of the south island of New Zealand. It was founded in 1864 on the strength of its gold rush, and within a few short years was one of New Zeakand's largest towns. Now it is known for its eco-tourism.
www.hokitika.org/

Mountain Jade Backpackers, 41 Weld St, Hokitika, NZ; T:037555185, *stay@ mountainjadebackpackers.co.nz/*; $21bed, Kitchen:Y, B'fast:N, WiFi:Y, Pvt. room:Y, Locker:N, Recep:ltd; Note: bike rent, tour desk, prkng, laundry, wh/chair ok, luggage rm

Birdsong Backpackers, 124 Kumara Jct. Hwy, Hokitika, NZ; T:037557179, *info@ birdsong.co.nz/*; $24bed, Kitchen:Y, B'fast:N, WiFi:Y, Pvt.room:Y, Locker:N, Recep:ltd; Note: tour desk, parking, laundry

INVERCARGILL is a city of over 50,000 residents at the southern tip of New Zealand. It has seen both secessionist and prohibitionist sentiments in its history; sounds like y'all-know-where. The dairy industry is a key factor in the town's economy.
www.invercargill.org.nz/

Sparkys Backpackers, 271 Tay St, Invercargill, NZ; *sparkysbackpackers. co.nz/*; T:032172905, *sparkysbackpackers@hotmail.com*; $21bed, Kitchen:N, B'fast:Y, WiFi:Y, Pvt.room:Y, Locker:N, Recep:ltd; Note: bar, hot tub, laundry, parking

KAIKOURA is a town of a couple thou on the northern end of the south island's east coast. The marine life deriving from the proximity of the nearby underwater Hikurangi Trench is crucial to the town's history and livelihood, first as a whaling station, and more recently as a tourist destination for whale-watching, swimming with dolphins, and seal colony observation. It is connected by train to Christchurch and northern ferries.

www.kaikoura.nz.com/

Dolphin Lodge Backpackers, 15 Deal St, Kaikoura, NZ; *dolphinlodge. co.nz/*, T:+64/33195842, *dolphinlodge@xtra.co.nz*; $23bed, Kitchen:Y, B'fast:N, WiFi:Y, Pvt.room:Y, Locker:N, Recep:ltd; Note: spa, log fire, parking, laundry, tour desk, c.c. ok, safe dep

Albatross Backpackers' Inn, 1 Torquay St, Kaikoura, NZ; *albatross-kaikoura.co.nz/*, T:0800222247, *albatrossnz@xtra.co.nz*; $24bed, Kitchen:N, B'fast:N, WiFi:N, Pvt.room:Y, Locker:N, Recep:ltd; Note: bikes, activities, parking, tour desk, laundry, c.c. ok, curry nite

YHA Kaikoura, 270 Esplanade, Kaikoura, NZ; T:+64/33195931, *yha. kaikoura@   yha.co.nz/*; $25bed, Kitchen:Y, B'fast:N, WiFi:Y, Pvt.room:Y, Locker:N, Recep:9a>8p; Note: nr sea, tour desk, parking, laundry, wh/chair ok, c.c. ok

LAKE TEKAPO is a lake in the center of New Zealand's south island, with an area of 32sq.mi/83sq.km at an elevation of 2300ft/700mt above sea level. The dam provides hydroelectric power.

www.tekapotourism.co.nz/

YHA Tekapo, 3 Simpson Lane, Lake Tekapo, NZ; T:+64/36806857, *yha. laketekapo@   yha.co.nz/*; $24bed, Kitchen:Y, B'fast:N, WiFi:Y, Pvt.room:Y,

Locker:Y, Recep:ltd; Note: free SIM card, tour desk, parking, laundry, wh/chair ok, c.c. ok

METHVEN is a small town of a thousand or so in the center of the south island in the Canterbury region. With little more than hot-air ballooning to do in summer, Mount Hutt and its skifield are nearby to liven the place up in winter.

www.amazingspace.co.nz/

Big Tree Lodge, 25 S Belt, Methven, NZ; *bigtreelodge.co.nz/*, T:033029575, *bigtree@xtra.co.nz*; $25bed, Kitchen:Y, B'fast:N, WiFi:Y, Pvt.room:Y, Locker:Y, Recep:ltd; Note: parking, laundry, c.c. ok, luggage room, wood fire, ski locker

MOUNT COOK is New Zealand's highest peak, at 12,300ft/3750mt, located in the Southern Alps of the south island's western rim. Its four national parks comprise a world heritage site, featuring peaks and glaciers and some good mountain climbing. The village is base camp, seven clicks from Tasman Glacier and twelve from the summit.

www.mtcooknz.com/

YHA Mount Cook, Cnr BowenKitchener, Mount Cook Village, NZ; T:+64/34351820, *yhamtck@ yha.co.nz/*; $30bed, Kitchen:Y, B'fast:N, WiFi:Y, Pvt.room:Y, Locker:N, Recep:9a>7p; Note: tour desk, parking, laundry, wh/chair ok, c.c. ok, luggage rm

OAMARU is a town of 13,000 on the east coast of the south island, known for its important archeological sites. The town has a historic district, also, made of the local 'Oamaru' limestone. There are unique local penguins, also.

www.visitoamaru.co.nz/home.aspx

Chillawhile Backpackers Art Gallery, 1 Frome St, Oamaru North, NZ; T:+64(03)4370168, *stay@ chillawhile.co.nz/*; $27bed, Kitchen:Y, B'fast:N, WiFi:Y, Pvt.room:Y, Locker:N, Recep:>9p; Note: parking, luggage room, laundry, c.c. ok, historical bldg/town

Empire Backpackers, 13 Thames St, *empirebackpackersoamaru.co.nz/*, T:(03)4343446, *empirebackpackers@gmail.com*; $23bed, Kitchen:Y, B'fast:Y, WiFi:Y, Pvt.room:Y, Locker:Y, Recep:ltd; Note: billiards, old-fashioned, parking, laundry, central, penguins, beach

PICTON is a town of almost 3000 on the north end of the south island, and is the terminal for the ferry from Wellington. Thus it is the most important transportation link between the north and south islands.
www.picton.co.nz

Sequoia Lodge, 3 Nelson Square, Picton, NZ; T:+64(03)5738399, *stay@ sequoialodge.co.nz/*; $22bed, Kitchen:Y, B'fast:N, WiFi:Y, Pvt.room:Y, Locker:N, Recep:ltd; Note: parking, laundry, cake/ice cream, ferry/train shuttle, free 50MB

Fat Cod Backpackers, 9 Auckland St, Picton, NZ; T:+64/35737788, *info@ fatcodbackpackers.co.nz/*; $21bed, Kitchen:N, B'fast:N, WiFi:Y, Pvt.room:Y, Locker:$, Recep:ltd; Note: parking, tour desk, laundry, c.c. ok, near ferry & train

YHA Anakiwa Lodge, 9 Lady Cobham Grove, Anakiwa, RD1 Picton; *yha.co.nz/*, T:+64/35742115, *info@anakiwa.co.nz*; $26bed, Kitchen:Y, B'fast:Y, WiFi:Y, Pvt.room:Y, Locker:N, Recep:8a-10p; Note: kayaks, tour desk, parking, laundry, luggage rm, far, hot tub

QUEENSTOWN is a resort town in the far south of the country, best known for its mountain-sports tourism, and the making of the "Lord of the Rings" trilogy. With nearby towns it forms a lakes district, with a resident population of 29,000, over half of those in Queenstown ward. It fancies itself 'Adventure Capital of the World.' There is an international jazz festival.
www.queenstownnz.co.nz

Absoloot Value Accommodation, 50 Beach St, Queenstown, NZ; T:+64(03)4429522, *info@ absoloot.co.nz/*; $22bed, Kitchen:Y, B'fast:N, WiFi:Y, Pvt.room:Y, Locker:Y, Recep:ltd; Note: lift, tour desk, parking, free WiFi, laundry, a/c, c.c. ok, central

YHA Queenstown Lakefront, 88-90 Lake Esplanade, Queenstown, NZ; *queenstown.lakefront@ yha.co.nz/*, T+64/34428413, TF:0800278299; $24bed, Kitchen:Y, B'fast:N, WiFi:$, Pvt.room:Y, Locker:N, Recep:7a>10p; Note: not central, wheelchair ok, tour desk, luggage rm, laundry, parking

YHA Queenstown Central, 48A Shotover St, Queenstown, NZ; T:+64/34427400, *yha.queenstowncentral@ yha.co.nz/*; $32bed, Kitchen:Y, B'fast:N, WiFi:$, Pvt.room:Y, Locker:N, Recep:>10p; Note: tour desk, luggage room, laundry, central, nr bus, games, TV

Bumbles Backpackers Queenstown, Cnr Lake Esplanade/Brunswick St; T:034426298, *stay@ bumblesbackpackers.co.nz/*; $24bed, Kitchen:Y, B'fast:N, WiFi:$, Pvt.room:N, Locker:$, Recep:>7p; Note: tour desk, luggage rm, laundry, central, c.c. ok

Adventure Queenstown Hostel, 36 Camp St, Queenstown, NZ; T:+64(03)4090862, *reception@ aqhostel.co.nz/*; $24bed, Kitchen:Y, B'fast:N, WiFi:Y, Pvt.room:N, Locker:Y, Recep:ltd; Note: bike rent, tour desk, laundry, luggage room, a/c, c.c. ok

Pinewood Lodge, 48 Hamilton Road, Queenstown, NZ; T:+64(03)4428273, *booking@ pinewood.co.nz/*; $25bed, Kitchen:Y, B'fast:N, WiFi:Y, Pvt.room:Y, Locker:N, Recep:>9p; Note: tour desk, luggage room, laundry, close, c.c. ok, parking, bike rent

Reavers Lodge, 56 Hamilton Road, Queenstown, NZ; *reavers.co.nz/*, T:+64(03)4411059, *info@ozsnowadventures.com.au*; $22bed, Kitchen:N, B'fast:Y, WiFi:Y, Pvt.room:Y, Locker:N, Recep:ltd; Note: wheelchair ok, tour desk, laundry, luggage room, parking, c.c. ok

Base Queenstown, 47-49 Shotover Street, Queenstown, NZ; T:+64(03)4411185, *queenstown@ stayatbase.com/*; $23bed, Kitchen:Y, B'fast:$, WiFi:Y, Pvt.room:Y, Locker:Y, Recep:24/7; Note: resto/bar, wheelchair, ok, party, tour desk, c.c. ok, central, bar noise

TE ANAU is a town on the lake of the same name in the far south of the south island. It is the gateway to Fjordland National Park. There are caves, too.
www.fiordland.org.nz

YHA Te Anau, 29 Mokonui St, Te Anau, NZ; T:+64/32497847, *yha. teanau@ yha.co.nz/*; $24bed, Kitchen:Y, B'fast:N, WiFi:Y, Pvt.room:Y, Locker:N, Recep:9a>7p; Note: tour desk, parking, laundry, wh/chair ok, c.c. ok

WANAKA is a town in the far south Otago region of the southern island, located on the southern end of Lake Wanaka and the gateway to Mount Aspiring National Park. Originally settled during the 19th century gold rushes, today it is largely devoted to tourism, specializing in outdoor recreation, including hiking, biking, fishing, and more. In the winter it provides access to winter parks and ski resorts.
www.lakewanaka.co.nz/

Hollys Backpacker, 71 Upton St, Wanaka, NZ; *hollys-backpacker.co.nz/*, T:034438187, *hollys@xtra.co.nz*; $23bed, Kitchen:Y, B'fast:N, WiFi:Y, Pvt. room:Y, Locker:N, Recep:ltd; Note: tour desk, parking, laundry, close to center, mountain view

Base Wanaka, Level 1, 73 Brownston St, Wanaka, NZ; T:+64/34434291, *wanaka@ stayatbase.com/*; $22bed, Kitchen:Y, B'fast:N, WiFi:Y, Pvt.room:Y, Locker:Y, Recep:ltd; Note: resto/bar, parking, laundry, wh/chair ok, tour desk, central

Part III: Pacific Islands

11) Brunei

Brunei's is the only independent country on the island of Borneo. Its history more or less parallels that of Funan, Srivijaya, and the Majapahit kingdoms of SE Asia and Indonesia, until the arrival of Islam and the expansion of the Brunei Empire to include all of northern Borneo, including Sabah and Sarawak, the Sulu archipelago, and the area that is modern-day Manila. It lost heavily against Spain, then broke off piece by piece to keep the British at bay. It became a British protectorate in 1888 until 1984. Meanwhile oil was discovered and today Brunei is the second-richest country in SE Asia after Singapore. It has a population of 400,000 of which almost half are in the capital of Bandar Seri Begawan. Two-thirds of the population are ethnic Malay...and Muslim. The rest are Chinese and indigenous, Buddhist and Christian. The law is sharia; i.e. alcohol is verboten. The language is Malay. The currency is the Brunei dollar (BND). The phone code is +673.

Sumbiling Eco Village, Kg Sumbiling Lama, Jl. Batang Duri, Temburong; *sumbiling.blogspot.com/*, T:+673/2426923, +673/8766796, *sales@borneoguide. com* $43Tent, Pvt.room:Y, Kitchen:N, B'fast:$, WiFi:N, Locker:Y, Recep:ltd; Note: national park/rainforest, parking

Pusat Belia, Jl. Sungai Kianggeh, Bandar Seri Begawan, Brunei; *youthhostel.551@hotmail.com*, T:+673/2223936, *jimy5192@hotmail.com, jbsbelia@ brunet.bn*; $10Bed, Pvt.room:N Kitchen:N, B'fast:N, WiFi:$, Locker:N, Recep:ltd; Note: not bookable/show up, downtown

12) Cook Islands

The Cook Islands are a self-governing colony in free association with New Zealand, composed of fifteen islands in the South Pacific. They are inhabited by Polynesians who first arrived in the 6th century. Dialects closely related to Maori and Samoan are spoken. Traditional crafts include carving, weaving, and *tivaevae* – scenery quilts. There are top-notch New Zealand-trained contemporary artists, too. Phone code is +682. Currency is the New Zealand dollar (NZD) and the Cook Islands dollar. Languages are English, Maori, and tribal dialects.

RAROTONGA is the most populous of the Cook Islands, with almost three-fourths of the islands' 20,000 inhabitants. The island is 26 sq.mi/67sq.km in area. Avarua is the capital of both the island and the country. Tourism is the main industry, beaches the main attraction. There is also a cross-island hike.
www.cookislands.travel/rarotonga

Backpackers Intl. Hostel, PO 878, Rarotonga, Cook Islands; *backpackersinternational.com/*, T:+682/21847, *annabill@backpackers.co.ck;* $15bed, Kitchen:Y, B'fast:N, WiFi:$, Pvt.room:Y, Locker:N, Recep:ltd; Note: arpt pickup, laundry, parking, c.c. ok, basic, SW coast, free fruit

Vara's Beach House, PO Box 434, Muri Beach, Ngatangiia, Rarotonga; T:+682/23156, *stay@ varasbeach.co.ck/*; $20bed, Kitchen:Y, B'fast:N, WiFi:Y, Pvt.room:Y, Locker:N, Recep:ltd; Note: pickup $, parking, tour desk, c.c. ok, near beach, no towels

Tiare Village, P.O. Box 719, Atupa, Rarotonga, Cook Islands; T:+682/23466, *kiaorana@ tiarevillage.co.ck/*; $16bed, Kitchen:Y, B'fast:N, WiFi:Y, Pvt.room:Y, Locker:N, Recep:ltd; Note: free tour, min 2N, 3km> Avarua, pool no beach, luggage ok, bikes

Atupa Orchid Units, PO Box 64, Rarotonga, Cook I; T:+682/28543, *ingrid@ atupaorchids.co.ck/*; $20bed, Kitchen:Y, B'fast:N, WiFi:N, Pvt.room:Y, Locker:N, Recep:24/7; Note: cash, laundry, tour desk, walk to town/beach

13) Easter Island/Rapa Nui (Chile)

EASTER ISLAND is the most remote island on earth, its closest inhabited neighbor some 1300mi/2100km to the west, and it the southeasternmost point of the Polynesian Triangle that also includes and is defined by Hawaii and New Zealand. It is famous for its 887 hand-carved and humongous *moai* statues and speculation as to how they were built and why they stopped being built, all the more perplexing since it all happened a short few hundred years ago, apparemtly since the first Western visitors. They created the only Polynesian script, *rongorongo*. The islands were annexed by Chile in 1888. Tourism is the only industry. The population is almost 6000. Currency is Chile's peso (CLP). Languages are Spanish and *rapa nui*. Calling code is +56.
www.netaxs.com/

Residencial Vaianny, Tuki Haka He Vari, Easter Island, Chile; *residencialvaianny.com/*, T:0322100650; $30bed, Kitchen:Y, B'fast:Y, WiFi:Y Pvt. room:Y, Locker:N, Recep:ltd; Note: laundry, tour desk, central

Kona Tau, Avaraipau s/n, Easter Island, **Chile**; *hihostels.com/*, T:+56322100321, *konatau@entelchile.net*; $35bed, Kitchen:Y, B'fast:Y, WiFi:Y, Pvt.room:Y, Locker:Y, Recep:24/7; Note: arpt pickup, tour desk, parking, laundry, luggage room, cash only

14) Fiji

FIJI is an island nation of some 332 islands — 110 inhabited — covering an area of some 7000sq.mi/18,000sq.km and home to some 850,000 souls in the south Pacific. It is ethnically and linguistically Melanesian, presumably Austronesian language and culture superimposed upon a preexisting aboriginal racial type. If this all got its start three to five thousand years ago, it enters the pages of modern history with the arrival of the Dutch and British in the 17th and 18th centuries. The British stayed until 1970. For that they are today one of the most developed countries of the region. The main problem is how to share power between native Fijians and more recent Indian immigrants and mixed-bloods.

In general these days the Indians run the economy; the locals run the government and arned forces. That's AFTER several coups; when an Indian got elected Prime Minister in 1997 all Hell broke loose. Indians are now immigrating to elsewhere in a noticeable stream. Fiji maintains a fairly large and efficient military by the way. As long as there is ethnic tension, they will likely control things. To keep things peaceful is good for tourism, which is the only real industry, aside from sugar. Despite its complications, it could be worse, as is the case with most of the other islands of the South Pacific. Fiji is in many ways the saving grace of the South Pacific — cheap, diverse, and friendly, with a good choice of amenities and options for all budgets. You'd have to go to Tahiti or Hawaii to find things more efficiently run, and those places aren't cheap. Fiji is.

For a quickie trip or brief stopover, it's hard to beat the main island of Viti Levu surrounding the international airport at Nadi for price and convenience. For longer trips the Yasawa Islands and elsewhere rate highly, for a price. Many islands in fact are pretty much self-contained compounds and meal plans are required in what may seem at first glance like very cheap prices for a bed. WiFi may be expensive if available at all, so better check first if required, regardless of what it says here. Many of the usual specs and details will be useless for these island compounds. Some islands have little or nothing else. Others are closer to the main island, and if you don't mind toting groceries, offer self-catering. Calling code is +679. Languages are English, Hindi, and Fijian.

www.fijime.com/

14) Fiji

BEACHCOMBER ISLAND is a marine sanctuary in the Mamanuca Islands, just 11mi/17km from the international airport at Nadi.

Beachcomber Island Resort, Beachcomber Island, Fiji; T:+679/6661500, *info@ beachcomberfiji.com/*; $28bed, Kitchen:N, B'fast:N, WiFi:N, Pvt.room:Y, Locker:Y, Recep:ltd; Note: resto/club, arpt trans, laundry, luggage rm, forex, tour desk, basic

BOUNTY ISLAND is 48 acres of tourist resort only 15 minutes from Nadi airport.

Bounty Island Sanctury Resort, Lautoka, Bounty Island, Fiji; *fiji-bounty. com/*, T:+679/6283387, *sales@bounty.com.fi*; $40bed, Kitchen:N, B'fast:N, WiFi:N, Pvt.room:Y, Locker:N, Recep:ltd; Note: meal pkg, pool, games, activities, laundry

CORAL COAST is a strand of sand along the southwestern side of the main island Viti Levu between Nadi and Suva.
www.coralcoastfiji.com/

Beachouse Backpackers, Korolevu, Coral Coast, Viti Levu; TF:(AU)800666237, *bookings@ nomadsworld.com/*; $26bed, Kitchen:Y, B'fast:Y, WiFi:N, Pvt.room:Y, Locker:N, Recep:ltd; Note: pool, kayaks, treks, horses, village visits, café/bar

Tubakula Beach Bungalows, Sigatoka, Coral Coast, Fiji; T:+679/6500097, *tubakula@ fiji4less.com/*; $16bed, Kitchen:Y, B'fast:$, WiFi:N, Pvt.room:Y, Locker:N, Recep:ltd; Note: pool, forex, tour desk, meals

Namuka Bay Lagoon, Nadi, Coral Coast, Fiji; T:06700243, *info@ namukabayresort.com/*; $17bed, Kitchen:N, B'fast:N, WiFi:Y, Pvt.room:Y, Locker:Y, Recep:24/7; Note: resto/bar, arpt trans, laundry, luggage rm, forex, wh/chair ok

LAUTOKA is the second largest city of Fiji, with more than 50,000 inhabitants. As the traditional center of the sugar industry, ethnic Indians predominate here. It is situated north of Nadi on the main island of Viti Levu. The sugar mill and botanical gardens are worth a check.
tropicalfiji.com/sights_and_activities/scenic_highlights/lautoka.asp/

Cathay Hotel, Tavewa Ave, Lautoka, Fiji; *fiji4less.com/cathay/*, T:+679/6660566, *cathay@fiji4less.com*; $16bed, Kitchen:N, B'fast:N, WiFi:N, Pvt.room:Y, Locker:N, Recep:24/7; Note: resto/bar, parking, pool, forex, venerable old establishment

LELEUVIA ISLAND is a coral cay in the Lamaiviti archipelago. It has a resort.

Leleuvia Island Resort, 12 Nukuwatu St, Lami, Leleuvia Island, Fiji; T:+679/8384365, *reservations@ leleuvia.com/*; $39bed, Kitchen:N, B'fast:Y, WiFi:Y, Pvt.room:Y, Locker:N, Recep:ltd; Note: meals included, resto/bar, billiards

MALOLO ISLAND

Funky Fish Beach Resort, Malolo Island, Fiji; T:06282333, *enquiries@ funkyfishresort.com/*; $71bed, Kitchen:N, B'fast:N, WiFi:Y, Pvt.room:Y, Locker:N, Recep:ltd; Note: resto/bar, arpt trans, laundry, pool, tour desk, surf, meals included

MANA ISLAND

Ratu Kini DiveResort, Mana Island, Fiji; *ratukinidiveresort.com.fj/*, T:+679/6721959, *rtkinihostel@connect.com.fj*; $24bed, Kitchen:N, B'fast:Y, WiFi:Y, Pvt.room:Y, Locker:Y, Recep:ltd; Note: arpt p-u, resto/bar, a/c, tour desk

Mana Lagoon Backpackers, Mamanuca group, Mana Beach; T:+679/9246573, *manalagoonbackpackers.com/*,$24bed, Kitchen:N, B'fast:Y, WiFi:N, Pvt.room:N, Locker:N, Recep:24/7; Note: arpt p-u, luggage rm, café, tour desk, boat to Nadi, meals

NADI is where your plane will land from overseas, and there are scads of hostels a short drive away, forming a little colony down on the beach. There are many others a little farther away. The town itself is not bad, either, accessible by bus.

Travellers Beach Resort, Lot 19, Wasawasa RD, New Town, Nadi Bay; *travellersbeachresortfiji.com/,* T:+679/6723322; $12bed, Kitchen:N, B'fast:Y, WiFi:$, Pvt.room:Y, Locker:Y, Recep:24/7; Note: Kava Wed, free arpt p-u, bar, parking, forex, pool, wheelchair ok

Nomads Skylodge, Queens Highway, Nadi, Fiji; TF:(AU)800666237, *bookings@ nomadsworld.com/;* $9bed, Kitchen:Y, B'fast:N, WiFi:Y, Pvt.room:Y, Locker:Y, Recep:24/7; Note: resto/bar, c.c. ok, laundry, tour desk, pool, free arpt p-u

Stoney Creek Resort Fiji, Sabeto, Nadi, Fiji; *stoneycreekfiji.net/,* T:+6722206; $19bed, Kitchen:N, B'fast:Y, WiFi:N, Pvt.room:Y, Locker:Y, Recep:ltd; Note: hills no beach, resto/bar, parking, pool, hot tub, bikes, far

Smuggler's Cove, Nadi Bay, Nadi, Fiji; *smugglersbeachfiji.com/,* T:+679/6726579, *reservations@smugglerscove;* $12bed, Kitchen:N, B'fast:Y, WiFi:$, Pvt.room:Y, Locker:Y, Recep:24/7; Note: arpt p-u, resto/bar, a/c, c.c. ok, pool, TV, bikes, ATM, forex, laundry

Wailoaloa Beach Resort Fiji, Newtown Rd, Nadi Bay, Wailoaloa, Nadi; *wailoaloabeachresortfiji.com/,* T:+679/6727130; $9bed, Kitchen:Y, B'fast:Y, WiFi:Y, Pvt.room:Y, Locker:Y, Recep:24/7; Note: free arpt p-u, resto/bar, a/c, c.c. ok, walk>beach 10 min, tour desk

Beach Escape Villas, Newtown Beach, Nadi, Fiji; *beachescapefiji.com/,* T:+679/6724442, *beachescape@connect.com.fj;* $9bed, Kitchen:Y, B'fast:$, WiFi:$, Pvt.room:Y, Locker:N, Recep:24/7; Note: arpt p-u, resto/bar, forex, pool, luggage ok, laundry, a/c, c.c. ok

Horizon Beach Resort, Wailoaloa Beach, Nadi Bay, Fiji; *horizonbeachfiji. com/;* T:+679/6722832; $6bed, Kitchen:Y, B'fast:Y, WiFi:Y, Pvt.room:Y, Locker:N, Recep:24/7; Note: arpt p-u, resto/bar, a/c, c.c. ok, forex, left luggage, laundry

Seashell@Momi, Nadi, Fiji Islands; *seashellresort.com/*, T:(679)6706100, *seashell@connect.com.fj*;$14bed,Kitchen:N,B'fast:$,WiFi:Y,Pvt.room:Y,Locker:N, Recep:ltd; Note: resto/bar, parking, pool, left luggage, c.c. ok, tour desk

Nadi Bay Resort Hotel, Wailoaloa Beach Rd, Nadi; *fijinadibayhotel.com/*, T:(679)6723599, *nadibay@connect.com.fj*; $21bed, Kitchen:N, B'fast:Y, WiFi:Y, Pvt.room:Y, Locker:N, Recep:24/7; Note: arpt p-u, resto/bar, forex, tour desk, a/c, c.c. ok, laundry, luggage

Aquarius On The Beach, 17 Wasawasa Rd, Nadi, Fiji; T:+679/6726000, *reservations@ aquariusfiji.com/*; $18bed, Kitchen:N, B'fast:$, WiFi:Y, Pvt.room:Y, Locker:N, Recep:24/7; Note: arpt p-u, resto/bar, tour desk, c.c. ok, pool, beach

Jet Set Accommodation, Palm Rd, New Town, Nadi, Fiji; T:+679/6728750, *mailbox@ jetsetaccommodation.com/*; $20bed, Kitchen:N, B'fast:Y, Pvt. room:Y, Locker:N, Recep:24/7; Note: resto, luggage ok, arpt trans, wheelchair ok, basic, nr runway

Capricorn International, Queens Road, Martintar, Nadi, Fiji; *capricornfiji. com/*, T:+679/6720088, *capricorn@connect.com.fi*; $20bed, Kitchen:N, B'fast:Y, WiFi:Y, Pvt.room:N, Locker:Y, Recep:24/7; Note: resto/bar, billiards, arpt trans, luggage rm, forex, parking, pool

The Blue Bure, 10 Narewa Rd, Nadi, Fiji; *fijibluebure.com/*, T:6707030, *thebluebure@connect.com.fi*; $15bed, Kitchen:N, B'fast:Y, WiFi:Y, Pvt.room:Y, Locker:N, Recep:ltd; Note: resto/bar, parking, tour desk, luggage room

Saweni Beach Apts & Hotel, Saweni Beach, Nadi, Fiji; T:+679/6661777, *saweni@ fiji4less.com/*; $13bed, Kitchen:Y, B'fast:N, WiFi:N, Pvt.room:Y, Locker:N, Recep:>10p; Note: resto/bar, parking, tour desk, basic

PACIFIC HARBOR occupies a stretch of beach on the Coral Coast on the main island Viti Levu.

The Uprising Beach Resort, Beach Rd, Pac Harbour, *Fiji*; **T:(679)3452200,** *enquiries@ uprisingbeachresort.com/*; $22bed, Kitchen:N, B'fast:Y, WiFi:$, Pvt.

room:Y, Locker:Y, Recep:24/7; Note: resto/bar/club, parking, a/c, c.c. ok, laundry, left luggage, pool

Club Oceanus, P.O Box 400, Pacific Harbour, *Fiji*; T:679/3450498, *info@ cluboceanus/*; $21bed, Kitchen:N, B'fast:Y, WiFi:Y, Pvt.room:N, Locker:Y, Recep:24/7; Note: resto/bar, arpt trans, bikes, luggage rm, billiards, wh/ chair ok

QAMEA ISLAND

Maqai Beach, Matei, Qamea Island, *Fiji* Islands; *ojb.co.nz/*, T:+679/8503488, *maqaibeach@gmail.com*; $15bed, Kitchen:N, B'fast:N, WiFi:Y, Pvt.room:Y, Locker:N, Recep:ltd; Note: resto/bar, arpt trans, tour desk, eco-resort

RAKIRAKI is an agricultural area on Viti Levu's northern coast.

Bethams Beach Cottages, Rakiraki, *Fiji*; *bethams.com.fj/*, T:+679/6280400, *bethams@connect.com.fj*; $18bed, Kitchen:Y, B'fast:N, WiFi:N, Pvt.room:Y, Locker:N, Recep:ltd; Note: resto/bar, mini-market

ROBINSON CRUSOE ISLAND is a small island off the southwest coast of Fiji's main Viti Levu island. Prehistoric Lapita pottery has been found here.

Robinson Crusoe Island, Coral Coast, Fiji; *robinsoncrusoeislandfiji.com/*, T:+679/6281999; $27bed, Kitchen:N, B'fast:N, WiFi:Y, Pvt.room:N, Locker:N, Recep:ltd; Note: resto/bar, pool, tour desk, activities, kava, meal plans

SAVASAVU is a town located on Fiji's second island Vanua Levu, "Fiji's hidden paradise." It is known for its hotsprings and trade in exotic product— sandalwood, etc. Tourist draws include environmental and lifestyle programs, in addition to the usual beachy stuff.
www.fiji-savusavu.com/

Savusavu Hot Springs Hotel, Savusavu, Savusavu, Fiji; *hotspringsfiji.com/*, T:+679/8850195; $22bed, Kitchen:N, B'fast:$, WiFi:Y, Pvt.room:Y, Locker:N, Recep:ltd; Note: resto/bar, parking, pool, wheelchair ok, laundry, luggage ok

SIGATOKA is a town of almost 10,000 on Viti Levu's south Coral Coast. There is a Hare Krishna temple, the Sigatoka Sand Dunes, and Kula Eco Park, with birds from all over.

Mango Bay Resort, Queens Hwy, Namatakula Tadrawai, Sigatoka; T:+679/6530069, *info@ mangobayresortfiji.com/*; $20bed, Kitchen:N, B'fast:Y, WiFi:Y, Pvt.room:Y, Locker:N, Recep:ltd; Note: resto/bar/club, parking, tour desk, c.c. ok, bonfire, isolated

Vakaviti, Korotogo, Sigatoka, Fiji; T:(679)6500526, *info@ vakaviti.com/*; $11bed, Kitchen:Y, B'fast:N, WiFi:Y, Pvt.room:Y, Locker:Y, Recep:24/7; Note: on bus route to town, laundry, tour desk, pool

SUVA is the capital and largest city of Fiji, and is located on the southeast coast of the island of the main island Viti Levu. The city proper has a population of about 85,000 and the metropolitan area twice that. It is a cosmopolitan multicultural center and one of the few important cities in third-world Oceania. *www.fijime.com/index.php/fijime/page/28*

Raintree Lodge, Princes Rd, Colo i Suva (opp. Police Post), Suva, Fiji; *raintreelodge.com/*, T:+679/3320562, *raintreelodge@connect.com*; $14bed, Kitchen:N, B'fast:$, WiFi:Y, Pvt.room:Y, Locker:Y, Recep:ltd; Note: resto/bar, forex, tour desk, laundry, luggage ok, c.c. ok, nature, bus

South Seas Private Hostel, 6 Williamson Rd, Suva; T:+679/3312296, *southseas@ fiji4less.com/*; $13bed, Kitchen:Y, B'fast:N, WiFi:N, Pvt.room:Y, Locker:N, Recep:7a-/-10p; Note: luggage rm, forex, central, "perennial favorite"

Colonial Lodge, 19 Anand St, Suva, Fiji; T:+679/3300655, *suzie@ coloniallodge.com.fj*; $12bed, Kitchen:Y, B'fast:N, WiFi:Y, Pvt.room:Y, Locker:N, Recep:ltd; Note: homestay, near bus, parking, meals available, luggage room

YASAWA ISLANDS are a group of six main islands, and twenty all totaled, in western Fiji. It was long a port-of-call for cruises in the region, but it wasn't opened to the resort business until 1987. Since then, it has gradually become a favorite of backpackers and budget travelers, offering some native cultural amenitites in addition to the usual fun 'n sun. Due to the absence of commercial establishments, meals must generally be purchased as part of a full-board accommodation package.

Coralview Island Resort, Tavewa I., Yasawa Islands, Fiji; *coralview.com. fj/*, T:+679/6662648, *info@coral.com.fj*; $12bed, Kitchen:Y, B'fast:Y, WiFi:Y, Pvt. room:Y, Locker:N, Recep:ltd; Note: resto/bar, laundry, wheelchair ok, remote, meal $ obligatory

Barefoot Island Lodge, Naviti, Drawaqa Island, Yasawa Islands, Fiji; T:07763041, *info@ barefootislandfiji.com/*; $59bed, Kitchen:N, B'fast:Y, WiFi:Y, Pvt.room:Y, Locker:N, Recep:ltd; Note: resto/bar, c.c. ok, tour desk, meals included

Safe Landing Resort, Nacula Island, Yasawa I., Fiji; T:06230309, *enquiries@ safelandingfiji.com/*; $56bed, Kitchen:N, B'fast:N, WiFi:Y, Pvt.room:Y, Locker:N, Recep:ltd; Note: meals included, towel fee, resto/bar, tour desk, c.c. ok, partying

Mantaray Island Resort, Nanuya Balavu Island, Fiji; TF:(AU)800666237, *bookings@ nomadsworld.com/*; $24bed, Kitchen:Y, B'fast:$, WiFi:Y, Pvt.room:N, Locker:N, Recep:ltd; Note: meal plan $30+, kava, games, entertainment, TV, bar

Octopus Resort, LikuLiku Bay, Waya Island, Yasawa Islands, Fiji; T:+679/6030070, *reservations@ octopusresort.com/*; $24bed, Kitchen:N, B'fast:Y, WiFi:Y, Pvt.room:N, Locker:N, Recep:ltd; Note: meal plans, resto/bar, billiards, arpt trans, luggage rm, forex, pool

Blue Lagoon Beach Resort, Nacula Island, Yasawa Island Group, Fiji; *bluelagoonbeachresort.com.fj/*, T:+679/6030225, *reservations@ftn.net.nz*; $23bed, Kitchen:N, B'fast:N, WiFi:Y, Pvt.room:N, Locker:N, Recep:ltd; Note: meal plans, resto/bar, luggage rm, forex, tour desk, a/c, activities

Bay of Plenty Lodge, Matacawalevu Island, Yasawa Group, Fiji; T:+679/9023739, *info@ bayofplentyfiji.com/*; $48bed, Kitchen:N, B'fast:Y, WiFi:N, Pvt.room:Y, Locker:N, Recep:ltd; Note: meal plans, resto/bar, luggage room

Naqalia Lodge, Naqalia Pt, Wayalailai, Yasawa, Fiji; *naqalialodge-yasawa. com/*, T:+679/6240532, *naqalialodge@yahoo.com*; $48bed, Kitchen:N, B'fast:Y, WiFi:N, Pvt.room:N, Locker:N, Recep:ltd; Note: resto/bar, tour desk, arpt transfer, meals included

White SandyDive Beach Resort, Naviti Island, Yasawa, Fiji; *whitesandybeachresort.com/*, T:+679/6664066; $48bed, Kitchen:N, B'fast:Y, WiFi:N, Pvt.room:Y, Locker:N, Recep:ltd; Note: meals included, resto/bar, laundry, basic

Korovou Ecotour Resort, Yasawa, Fiji; *korovouecotourresort.com/*, T:6030049, *korovoultk@connect.com.fj*; $48bed, Kitchen:N, B'fast:Y, WiFi:Y, Pvt. room:Y, Locker:N, Recep:ltd; Note: meals included, resto/bar, pool, tour desk, activities, basic

15) French Polynesia

FRENCH POLYNESIA is an overseas territory of France, population 267,000, the most famous of which is Tahiti in the Society Islands group. The islands were settled by the Polynesians themselves since the beginning of the Common Era. The star Sirius was used for navigation... seriously. Magellan arrived in 1521. The French came in 1768. Unlike the Cook Islands or Micronesia, the relationship is not one of free association. They're fully French. The major export is black pearls. The main business is tourism. This is the fifth most developed economy in Oceania. Currency is the CFP franc. French and Tahitian are the languages. The calling code is +689.

15) French Polynesia

TAHITI is the largest of the islands in French Polynesia, one of the Society Islands in the windward group. It has a population of 178,000 — 68% of the total — and is the hub of all culture, commerce, and politics in the region. It was an independent kingdom until annexed by France in 1880. It is 2700mi/4400km south of Hawaii, 4900mi/7900km west of Chile, and 3500mi/5700km east of Australia. It is the island most responsible for the romanticism of island life by Europeans during their visits during the late 1700's. Today they are full French citizens. Papeete is the main city and residence of non-Polynesians. There is a traditional Heiva festival, a Gaugin museum, and a market for arts and crafts. There is a ferry to the nearby island of Moorea.

www.tahiti-tourisme.com/

Fare Suisse, BP 20255, Paofai, Tahiti, FP; T:+689/768121, *info@ fare-suisse.com/*; $52bed, Kitchen:Y, B'fast:$, WiFi:Y, Pvt.room:Y, Locker:N, Recep:24/7; Note: arpt pickup, pool table, tour desk, parking, bar, laundry, c.c. ok

Pension Te Miti, BP 130088 Punaauia, Moana Nui, Tahiti, FP; *pensiontemiti. com/*, T/F:(00689)584861, *pensiontemiti@mail.pf*; $27bed, Kitchen:Y, B'fast:Y, WiFi:$, Pvt.room:Y, Locker:Y, Recep:24/7; Note: arpt pickup, parking, luggage ok, c.c. ok, laundry, far from town

Taaroa Lodge, 6 Rue Albert Leboucher, Papeete, FP; *taaroalodge.com/*, T:+689/583921, *taaroalodge@mail.pf*; $29bed, Kitchen:Y, B'fast:Y, WiFi:N, Pvt. room:Y, Locker:N, Recep:ltd; Note: laundry, airport transfers

MOOREA is an island 11mi/17km from Tahiti and connected by ferry boat and airplane. There is a barrier reef.

Pension Motu Iti, BP 189 Maharepa Moorea, FP; *pensionmotuiti. com/*, T:(689)550520, *pensionmotuiti@mail.pf*; $20bed, Kitchen:N, B'fast:$, WiFi:Y, Pvt.room:Y, Locker:N, Recep:ltd; Note: resto, printer/scanner, free kayaks

16) Indonesia

Indonesia is a republic stretching across three time zones in the South Pacific and home to almost 240,000,000 people, fourth most populous in the world, residing on over 17,000 islands. Of the many islands and cultures comprised, Java and the Javanese dominate. It is one of the most densely populated areas in the world. It wasn't always dominant, though. The first stirrings of an Indonesian identity and strength were manifested with the Sriwijaya kingdom, located in Sumatra. The Malaysian race — closely related to the Indonesian — arose along the strait separating that island and what is now called Malaysia, a strait through which all inter-Ocean inter-Asian trade passed. The Majapahit kingdom of the 14th and 15th centuries shifted the focus over to Java. Hindu and Buddhist priests and scholars had long accompanied the kingdoms with their language and learning, but what happened next changed the identity of the region forever, as Muslim traders and proselytizers came in along the Malacca straits. They never left.

The European Christians came next in 1602, but never captured the hearts and minds of Indonesians, and exerted little control whatsoever, in fact until the 20th century, by which time colonialism was in decline. The Japanese moved in during WWII, and the locals declared independence when they left. Today Indonesia is the world's largest Muslim-majority nation, and struggling to keep it lite, out of the hands of fundamentalists. That's not easy, but economic development helps. That means China, and it seems to be working, with a growth rate over 6% recently, even during the 2008 world crisis. Chinese-Indonesians are a tiny and much-reviled segment of the total population, but they rule the country economically, as they do elsewhere in all Southeast Asian countries. Tourism is important, especially on the island of Bali. The food is tasty. The crafts are unsurpassed. But hostels are still in their infancy, limited mainly to Bali and a few places on Java. Indonesian Malay is the language, *rupiah* is currency; calling code is +62.

www.indonesia.travel/

BALI

Bali is the small island just east of Java and the center of Indonesian tourism, due mostly to its significant cultural differences from the rest of Indonesia. Firstly and most importantly, it's not Muslim. That means that you can do things here that you can't do elsewhere. That doesn't mean you'll get away with it, though. Indonesian society can be very conservative, which means, as elsewhere, that guys can do whatever they want; girls can't... unless they're tourists. Bali's got plenty of that, radiating outward from ground zero at Kuta Beach, a stone's throw from the international airport. Most of them are Aussies, doing the same things they do at home—surf, sun, sup—only cheaper. Bali's got culture, too, and art. This is where the old Hindu culture escaped to when the Muslims took over Java. Much of it is still here.

www.balitourismboard.org/

KUTA used to be a fishing village. It's not anymore. It's the Denpasar suburb closest to the international airport and the densest area for tourism on the island and in the country. It continues out in every direction, adding new villages to its tourist hustle and bustle: Legian, Seminyak, Kerobabkan, Canggu, Jimbaran, etc., shop after shop after club after club after restaurant after restaurant. It used to have a couple more, Paddy's and the Sari Club, blown up in 2002 about a week after I was there. I liked Paddy's, one of the few places that had something of a pub-like Thailandish feel to it, hard to find in Indonesia, even in Bali, which is non-Muslim. I remember some of the staff distinctly. They're all gone now. The beach-based bars of the mid-90's barely lasted a season. Still there's no shortage of entertainment here. It's just indoors and off the street.

Jolie Hostel, Jl. Uluwatu Raya GG Astina #23, Desa Ungasan, Jimbaran; T:+62/361704397, *contact@ joliehostel.com/*; $6bed, Kitchen:Y, B'fast:Y, WiFi:Y, Pvt.room:Y, Locker:Y, Recep:24/7; Note: pool, bikes, tour desk, laundry, luggage room, new

Ombak Bagus Homestay, Jl. Uma Sari 8, Banjar Babakan, Canggu, Bali; T:+62(0)81805504551, *info@ ombakbagus.com/*; $10bed, Kitchen:Y, B'fast:Y, WiFi:Y, Pvt.room:Y, Locker:N, Recep:ltd; Note: tea/coffee, laundry

Reinhold GH, Jl. Pengubugan, Banjar Silayukti, Kerobokan, Kuta Utara; T:081287159740, *contact.us@   thereinhold.com/*; $12bed, Kitchen:Y, B'fast:Y, WiFi:Y, Pvt.room:Y, Locker:N, Recep:24/7; Note: pool, bikes, forex, laundry, luggage room, safe deposit

Happy Day Hostel, Jalan Petitenget 100, Seminyak; *happydayhostel.com/*, T:+62/3617802777; $13bed, Kitchen:N, B'fast:Y, WiFi:Y, Pvt.room:N, Locker:Y, Recep:>10p; Note: parking, arpt trans, resto, a/c, c.c. +5%

Teka-teki Bali, Jl. Drupadi 1, Gg Puri Kubu #23, Seminyak; *tekatekibali. com/*, T:+62/3618475812, *tthouseinfo@gmail.com*; $16bed, Kitchen:N, B'fast:Y, WiFi:Y, Pvt.room:Y, Locker:Y, Recep:24/7; Note: tour desk, laundry, luggage room, a/c, parking, arpt trans, beach

The Island Hotel Bali, Jalan Padma Utara, Gang Abdi #18, Legian, Bali; T:0361762722, *reservations@ theislandhotelbali.com/*; $20bed, Kitchen:N, B'fast:Y, WiFi:Y, Pvt.room:Y, Locker:Y, Recep:ltd; Note: arpt p-u, resto/roofbar, laundry, alley, a/c, c.c. ok, pool, hotel

Kayun Hostel, Jl. Patih Jelantik 176 Legian, Kuta, Bali; T/F:+62/361752370, *reservations@ kayun-hostel.com/*; $20bed, Kitchen:N, B'fast:Y, WiFi:Y, Pvt. room:Y, Locker:Y, Recep:24/7; Note: pool, luggage rm, a/c, c.c. ok, games, nr beach/bars/clubs

Guess House Hostel, Petitenget St 22, Seminyak-Kuta, Bali; T:+62/3614730185, *info@ guesshousehostel.com/*; $13bed, Kitchen:Y, B'fast:Y, WiFi:Y, Pvt.room:Y, Locker:Y, Recep:ltd; Note: resto/bar, tour desk, ATM, forex, laundry, luggage rm, a/c, c.c.ok

Bed Bunkers Kuta, Jalan Dewi Sri 45 - 18, Kuta, Bali; T:+62/83114111120, *info@ bedbunkers.com/*; $11bed, Kitchen:N, B'fast:N, WiFi:Y, Pvt.room:N, Locker:Y, Recep:24/7; Note: forex, laundry, luggage room, a/c, parking, arpt trans, cozy

Echoland B&B Canggu Bali, Jl. Pantai Batu Mejan, Echo Beach, Bali; T:+62/3618870628, *info@ echolandbali.com/*; $18bed, Kitchen:N, B'fast:Y, WiFi:Y, Pvt.room:Y, Locker:Y, Recep:ltd; Note: TV, safe deposit, a/c

Grannys Hostel, Jl. Pura Martasari 28, Kuta, Bali; T:087861973112, *info@ grannyshostelandrestaurant.com/*; $12bed, Kitchen:N, B'fast:Y, WiFi:Y, Pvt.room:Y, Locker:Y, Recep:>11p; Note: resto/bar, tour desk, laundry, luggage room, a/c, not central

LOVINA is a stretch of beach west of Singaraja on the north coast, far quieter than the Kuta strand down south. It comprises several villages.

Bali Lovina Beach Cottage, Lovina, Singaraja Bali; T:036241285, *sales@ balilovinabeach.com/*; $35bed, Kitchen:N, B'fast:Y, WiFi:N, Pvt.room:Y, Locker:Y, Recep:ltd; Note: wh/chair ok, resto/bar, laundry, a/c, c.c. ok, pool, arpt trans, bikes

PADANG BAI is the small town where you can catch the ferry to Lombok and the Gili Islands. Or you can just enjoy small town Balinese life far from the madding crowds of Kuta.

Lemon House Bali, Jl Pelabuhan, Gang Melanting 5, Padang Bai, Bali; *lemonhousebali.com/*, T:081246371575, *lemonhousebali@gmail.com*; $10bed, Kitchen:N, B'fast:Y, WiFi:Y, Pvt.room:Y, Locker:N, Recep:ltd; Note: laundry, a/c, up hill w/ views, fishing village

Bamboo Paradise Bali, Jl Penataran Agung, Bali, *bambooparadisebali.com/*, T:082266304330, *bambooparadisebali@hotmail.com*; $9bed, Kitchen:N, B'fast:Y, WiFi:Y, Pvt.room:Y, Locker:Y, Recep:ltd; Note: tour desk, laundry, luggage room, a/c, café, arpt trans, beach

SANUR is the close-in alternative to Kuta, not far from the airport and Denpasar, but much quieter, yet still with bars and restos — more ex-pats than tourists.

Prima Cottage, Jalan Bumi Ayu, Sanur, Bali; *primacottage.com/*, T:0361286369; $13bed, Kitchen:N, B'fast:Y, Wi-Fi:Y, Pvt.room:Y, Locker:N, Recep:24/7; Note: wh/chair ok, resto/bar, laundry, pool, arpt trans, bikes

Big Pineapple B'packers Bali, Jl Tirta Ening Sanur Gang Blue Dive 5-6; *bigpineapple.hostel.com/*, T:+62/81805766160; $10bed, Kitchen:Y, B'fast:N, WiFi:$, Pvt.room:Y, Locker:Y, Recep:>8p; Note: dorm age limit 35, bike rent, TV, pool, forex, parking

Café Locca, Jl. Sudimala 5, Sanur, Bali; *cafelocca.com/*, T:+62/361283910; $10bed, Kitchen:Y, B'fast:Y, WiFi:Y, Pvt.room:Y, Locker:Y, Recep:ltd; Note: bar/café, bike rent, a/c, c.c. ok, tour desk, walk>beach

Java

Java is the world's most populous island, with 137 million folks, and one of the densest places on earth. Think Bangladesh. It is also the center of modern Indonesian culture, with its capital, predominant language and almost 60% of its people. It has distinct central, eastern, and western regions. Before all the humans, it had much wildlife.

BANDUNG is the country's third largest city, with a population of almost two and a half million, and is located in western Java some 110mi/180km south of Jakarta. At an elevation of 2500ft/750mt, it is cooler than other cities. A cultural hub, it is known as the "Paris of Indonesia."
bandungsae.com/

Hunny Hostel, Paskal Hyper Sq, blok C #28, Pasir Kaliki, Bandung, Java; *hunnyhostel.com/*, T:+(62)85862006722, *hunnyhostelbandung@yahoo.com*; $11bed, Kitchen:Y, B'fast:Y, WiFi:Y, Pvt.room:Y, Locker:Y, Recep:ltd; Note: tea/coffee, nr food stalls/cafes/etc, cash Rp only

JAKARTA is the capital of Indonesia and, with over ten million inhabitants, is 13th largest in the world. It's growing fast, too. The total conurbation has over twenty-eight million spread out over 250 sq.mi/650sq.km. It has appeared through history with many different names, before Jakarta being known by the Dutch and the world as Batavia. During that era it became a conglomerate of many different peoples and races with a culture and jargon of its own, still known today as Betawi. There are distinct Chinatowns, as Chinese people here don't assimilate genetically, and have been the object of much jealousy, prejudice, and violence. The food has been assimilated, however, and adds much to the cuisine. Hey, you gotta' have priorities.

As a modern global city, Jakarta has plenty of culture on hand. Festivals include Jakarta International Film Festival (JiFFest), Jakarta International Java Jazz Festival, Jakarta Fashion Week, Jakarta Fashion & Food Festival (JFFF), Jakarta Fair, Indonesia Creative Products, and Jakarta Arts and Crafts exhibition. Local institutions tend to be located around Merdeka (Freedom) Square and Old Town (Batavia). These include the National Museum of Indonesia, Monas (National Monument), Istiqlal Islamic Museum, Jakarta Cathedral Museum, Jakarta History Museum, the Wayang (Puppet) Museum, the Fine Art and Ceramic Museum, the Maritime Museum, Bank Indonesia Museum, and Bank Mandiri Museum. It's a monster city; enjoy.

www.jakarta-tourism.go.id/

Kamar-kamar for B'packers, Jl. RS Fatmawati #37 K, Jakarta Selatan; T:0217512560, *info@ kamar-kamar.com/*; $14bed, Kitchen:Y, B'fast:Y, WiFi:Y, Pvt.room:N, Locker:Y, Recep:ltd; Note: luggage $, parking, a/c, not central

Six Degrees, Jalan Cikini Raya, Jakarta, Java; T:+62(0)213141657, *jakarta-backpackers-hostel.com/*,; $13bed, Kitchen:Y, B'fast:Y, WiFi:Y, Pvt.room:Y, Locker:Y, Recep:24/7; Note: resto/bar, parking, laundry, games, a/c

Hunny Hostel, Jl Alaydrus, Jakarta Pusat; *hunnyhostel.com/*, T:02136135125, *hunnyhosteljakarta@yahoo.com*; $14bed, Kitchen:Y, B'fast:Y, WiFi:Y, Pvt. room:N, Locker:Y, Recep:ltd; Note: luggage room, laundry, parking, nr bus/train/MONAS, tea/coffee

Sunnydays YH, SudirmanPkApt, Tr A/GF, SteADAF1 Jl.Mansyur Kav35; T:02157942777, *sunnydays@ sunnydays-hostel.com/*; $20bed, Kitchen:N, B'fast:N, WiFi:Y, Pvt.room:N, Locker:Y, Recep:ltd; Note: not central, coffee/tea, resto, pool, a/c, ATM, shops

JOGJAKARTA is the cultural capital of Java and centre of classical Javanese fine art and culture, like batik, ballet, drama, music, poetry, and puppet shows. It retains a unique Javanese court Kraton culture, and Borobudur and Prambanan temple ruins are nearby, making it second only to Bali for tourism in Indonesia. It is alternately spelled and pronounced with 'j's or 'y's, one or the other, never mingled together.

www.jogjatourism.com/

Yogyakarta Backpacker, Purwodiningratan NG 1/915, Ngampilan, Jogja; *yogyakartabackpacker.wordpress.com*, T:0274514256, $6bed, Kitchen:Y, B'fast:N, *yogyakartabackpacker@yahoo.com*; WiFi:Y, Pvt.room:Y, Locker:N, Recep:ltd; Note: laundry, luggage rm, resto, gym

EDU Hostek Jogja, Jl Let Jen Suprapto No 17, Ngampilan, Yogyakarta; T:02748543295, *info@ eduhostels.com/*; $8bed, Kitchen:N, B'fast:Y, WiFi:Y,Pvt. room:Y, Locker:Y, Recep:24/7; Note: pool, parking, a/c, lift

Fuji Villa, Jl. Pelajar No. 8 Kaliurang, Yogyakarta; *fujivilla.blogspot.com/*, T/F:02748208777, *villafuji@yahoo.com*; $6bed, Kitchen:N, B'fast:Y, WiFi:Y, Pvt.room:Y, Locker:Y, Recep:ltd; Note: resto, wh/chair ok, tour desk, bikes, luggage room, parking

Venezia-homestay, Jl Tirtodipuran #27, Yogyakarta; T:0274374049, *booking@ venezia-homestay.com/*; $10bed, Kitchen:N, B'fast:N, WiFi:Y, Pvt. room:Y, Locker:N, Recep:ltd; Note: resto/bar, tour desk, laundry, mo'cy' rent, colonial style

SURABAYA, Java, is Indonesia's second-largest city with 2.7 million inhabitants, and lies on the northeast shore of Java, opposite the island of Madura, which reportedly has the prettiest women and meanest men in the country, no connection. There is now a bridge. The city has a cigarette meseum and a Chinese-style mosque dedicated to Zheng He. There is a Chinatown and an Arab town and the largest red-light district in SE Asia. Fun or fundamentalism? You decide.

www.surabayatourism.com/

IKIRU to Live, Jl. Ngagel Jaya Selatan III/3, Surabaya, Java; *ikiru-to-live. com/*, T:+62/3191706998, *ikiru.to.live@gmail.com*; $12bed, Kitchen:Y, B'fast:Y, WiFi:Y, Pvt.room:Y, Locker:N, Recep:ltd; Note: forex, tour desk, laundry, luggage room, a/c, parking

Da Rifi Hostel, Jl. Duku II/190, Pondok Candra, Surabaya; *darifi.hostel. com/*, T:+62/81334743870, *da_rifi@yahoo.co.id*; $8bed, Kitchen:N, B'fast:Y, WiFi:Y, Pvt.room:N, Locker:N, Recep:24/7; Note: resto, wheelchair ok, free tour/info, luggage rm, not central, nr arpt

Lombok

Lombok is the island to the immediate east of Bali and claims some of that culture — Hinduism, etc. — as its own. It also has traces of the wilder eastern culture.

GILI TRAWANGAN is the largest of the Gili Islands and has about 700 inhabitants. It is also the most developed of the Gilis, which pride themselves on their rustic and pristine nature — no motorized vehicles allowed. It is accessible from Bali and Lonbok by ferry. They say there are psilocybin mushrooms. I wouldn't know.
www.lombok-network.com/gili_islands/trawangan.htm

Mentigi Bay Floating Hotel, Gili Trawangan, Lombok; *mentigi-bay. com/*, T:+62/353292447, *mentigibay@hotmail.com*; $44bed, Kitchen:N, B'fast:Y, WiFi:N, Pvt.room:N, Locker:N, Recep:ltd; Note: resto, laundry, c.c. ok

Sulawesi

Sulawesi, formerly known as Celebes, is Indonesia's fourth-largest island and the world's eleventh. It is unusual in being composed of four peninsulas — the result of tectonic plate convergence — which give it something of a scorpion shape floating on the sea between Borneo and Maluku. It is renowned for its tribal Toraja architecture and has been the scene of Muslim-Christian violence in recent years. Population is over 17 million, and Makassar is the largest city.

TENTENA is a small town in central Sulawesi, located on Lake Poso and capital of North Pamona district, named after the local indigenous Pamona tribe. It is a predominantly Christian area that has previously seen violence with Muslims.

Ue Datu Lodge/Cottages, Ue Datu 92-93, Tentena-Poso, Palu, Sulawesi; *uedatucottages.com/*, T:+62/8113441597; $7bed, Kitchen:Y, B'fast:Y, WiFi:Y, Pvt. room:Y, Locker:N, Recep:24/7; Note: resto, forex, tour desk, bikes, luggage room, parking

Sumatra

Sumatra is the sixth-largest island in the world, home to over fifty million people. The westernmost of the Sunda Islands, it is bordered by the Malay peninsula to the east across the Strait of Malacca, with which it shares much culture and history. This is the location of the Buddhist Sriwijaya dynasty centered in Palembang in the 7th - 9th centuries and the point of introduction and diffusion of Islam in the 13th century. It is an active seismic zone, with constant volcanoes and earthquakes. It is also home to orangutans and many tribal groups. Medan is the largest city.
  www.sumatra.world-guides.com

PADANG is a city of more than 800,000 on the west coast and is a common transit point for surfers and backpackers on the way to the Batu Islands and Tentawai Islands. Among the locals, it's the place from which comes Indonesia's most famous cuisine, *nasi padang,* as formulated by the nearby tribal Minangkabau people, featuring coconut curries. อะไรว่า ?
  www.sumatra-indonesia.com/padang.htm

Brigette's House, Jl Kampung Sebelah 1 No 14d, Sumatra, Padang; *brigittehouse.blogspot.com/*, T:081374257162, *brigitte.house@yahoo.com*; $10bed,

Kitchen:N, B'fast:Y, WiFi:Y, Pvt.room:Y, Locker:N, Recep:24/7; Note: forex, laundry, luggage room

Timor

Timor is an island shared between the independent state of Timor L'este (East Timor) and Indonesian West Timor, part of the province of Nusa Tenggara. The people are mostly Papuan/Melanesian racially and speak Austronesian languages. The division comes from different colonial masters Holland and Portugal, the latter which only left in 1975, at which time Indonesia snatched it. After much strife, it finally became independent in 2002. The weavings are incredible, some of them dead ringers for Guatemalan. Go figure.

KUPANG, Timor, is a city of 350,000 on the Indonesian side of the divided island of Timor. It is the largest city and port. I hope you like fish.
www.tourismntt.com/timor.htm

Lavalon Hostel & Bar, Sumatera 44, Tode-Kisar, Kupang, Timor; *lavalontouristinfo.com/*, T:+62380832256, *lavalonbar@gmail.com*; $5bed, Kitchen:Y, B'fast:Y, WiFi:Y, Pvt.room:N, Locker:N, Recep:24/7; Note: resto/ bar, tour desk, laundry, luggage room, a/c, c.c. ok, basic

17) Marshall Islands

MARSHALL ISLANDS are a country of some 68,000 people on 1156 islands comprising thirty-four atolls. Most of them are around the capital and largest "city" Majuro. Settled in the second millennium BCE, Europeans arrived in 1526 and proceeded to make a mess of things. The Spanish were first, in the same round of expeditions that found and founded the Phillippines and

Guam. They sold it to Germany in 1884 and the Japanese snatched it in WWI, later to use it militarily in WWII. The US starved them out and occupied it in 1945, proceeding to use it to test nuclear weapons. Remember the song, "No Bikini Atoll?" Life goes on for the average Marshallese, fishing and f*cking. They became independent in 1986. The hardest part is getting here. English and Marshallese are the languages, US dollar is currency; phone code is +692.
   www.visitmarshallislands.com/

MAJURO is the name of the atoll and the city, 25-30,000 depending on how you count. The highest point is less than ten feet above sea level. Taiwanese run most of the businesses; the ratio of markets to shoppers is high.

   Flame Tree Backpackers, Mieco Beach Front, Amata Kabua Bl, Majuro, M.I; *journal@ntamar.net* T:+692/6254229; $15bed, Kitchen:Y, B'fast:$, WiFi:$, Pvt.room:Y, Locker:N, Desk hr: 24/7; Note: resto/bar, parking, arpt shuttle, dorms (mini-rooms) better than pvt

18) Papua New Guinea

PAPUA NEW GUINEA occupies the eastern portion of the large island of New Guinea, along with the Papua Province of Indonesia. With a population of seven million, it is one of the world's most interesting and diverse countries, and also one of its most dangerous. It has over 800 languages and as many cultures, mostly living on subsistence farming and wages of less than two dollars a day. It is generally considered one of the 'Melanesian' countries, though that applies mostly to the coastal areas, as the highlands and its Papuan cultures are considerably different. Languages are of one type or the other—Papuan or Melanesian—so for intercommunication between groups, a *lingua franca* must be used, most often *tok pisin* (Melanesian pidgin), but also *hiri* (police) *motu*, and English. Arts and crafts in the country are splendid, with Melanesians here one of the world's premier woodcarving groups, while the highland Papuans specialize in ornate body art.

Transportation is difficult, with no roads leading outward to anywhere from the capital Port Moresby. One of the few important roads connects Mt. Hagen in the highlands with Lae on the northern coast. Bandits apparently charge tolls along that road with impunity. This all started at least 50,000 years ago as people 'out of Africa' populated the island at more or less the same time as Australia, and by presumably some of the same groups of people, though there seems to be little evidence of intercommunication between the two, even when they were connected by a land bridge. Those people would correspond to today's Papuans in PNG and the Aborigines in Australia. More recently, some 4-5000 years ago seafaring Asians speaking Austronesian languages migrated into the area and formed the groups known today as Melanesian, Micronesian and Polynesian, in addition to the multifarious Indonesian groups, including the Malagasy off the coast of Africa.

Australia has been the major foreign influence, though Germany and Great Britain both played roles previously. A major campaign against Japan was fought here as part of WWII. It became independent in 1975 as a member of the Commonwealth. Despite extreme poverty, it is currently showing rapid growth, albeit much of it in controversial mining operations, many involving Chinese companies. Tourism is fledgling and best pursued in groups for safety and convenience. There aren't 'real' hostels in the modern sense, but real in the oldest sense – safe havens, most run by missionaries. Currency is the *kina* (PGK) and the calling code is +675. The place is expensive, too.

www.papuanewguinea.travel

PORT MORESBY is a city of over 300,000 people and the capital of the country. It is consistently ranked as one of the least liveable cities of the world. It has existed a scarce hundred years. It played an important role in the WWII Allied effort, as the last line of defense before Australia. This is the air hub for the country and the region. *Sal si puedes.*

Mapang Missionary Home, Lot 17, Sect. 25, Lahara Ave, Boroko, PNG; *office@mapang.org.pg*, T:6753404269; $60bed, Kitchen:Y, B'fast:Y, WiFi:$, Pvt. room:Y, Locker:N, Recep:ltd; Note: reserve no more than one week ahead (missionaries served first)

LAE is the second-largest city of the country and lies on the north coast at the terminus of the highlands highway. Every place of business has an armed guard. Watch your back.

Summer Institute of Linguistics GH, *rc-laeguesthouse@sil.org.pg;*
Kitchen:Y, B'fast:N, WiFi:N, Pvt.room:$50, Locker:N, Recep:ltd; Note: Budget room with shared kithchen & bathroom

19) Philippines

The Philippines is an oceanic nation of more than 7000 islands, off the Pacific east coast of SE Asia. With more than 100 million nationals – including overseas residents – the Phillippines is one of the most populous nations in the world and the fastest-growing outside Africa. Its history goes back more than 50,000 years with the arrival of the first *homo sapiens* from Africa, presumably ancestors of today's so-called 'negritos,' in the same waves that brought Papuans to New Guinea and Aborigines to Australia. Asian ancestors of today's ethnic 'Filipinos' came much later, Austronesian-speaking groups from Taiwan that today are represented by any of dozens of ethnicities that populate the archipelago.

Continual tricklings of seafaring ethnic Chinese and Arabs added some cultural thickener to the mix, but there wasn't much of a cohesive national identity until the arrival of Magallanes (Magellan) and the Spaniards with Catholicism in 1521. They stayed almost three hundred years, and only left to be replaced by the Americans after the Spanish-American War. They gained independence after WWII, and were ruled by dictator Ferdinad Marcos for almost two decades before 'People Power' deposed him and finally brought democracy. The challenges today are overpopulation and Islamic insurrection in the south. They call themselves "Pinoy." Hostels are in their infancy here, and still very much a novelty. Beware rooms with no windows. Official languages are Tagalog and English, currency the peso (PHP), calling code +63.
www.tourism.gov.ph/Pages/default.aspx

19) Philippines

BORACAY ISLAND is the shining jewel in the crown of the Phillippines' coastline, comparable to Phuket in Thailand or Bali in Indonesia, highly developed and commercialized to the max. As elsewhere, that doesn't mean it's bad. That just means you won't have the beach to yourself. They'd like to get their tourist numbers up as high as the region's others. The two primary tourism beaches are White Beach and Bulabog Beach, but the whole island's game. October to May has the best weather; storms in the Phillippines can be hellacious. Aquatic sports are the main activity.

www.boracayonline.com/

Frendz Resort, Nr Boat Stn 1, Balabag Main Beach, Boracay (Aklan); *frendzresortboracay.com/*, T:0362883803, *frendzresort@hotmail.com*; $12bed, Kitchen:N, B'fast:N, WiFi:Y, Pvt.room:Y, Locker:N, Recep:24/7; Note: resto/ bar, tour desk, forex, luggage rm, games, a/c, walk>beach

CEBU is a city and an island and a province, one of the most developed, and, in fact the oldest, in the Phillippines. The Spanish first came in 1521, but weren't able to defeat the local rajahs until 1565, thus founding Cebu. The Americans took over in 1898 and the Japanese occupied in WWII. Since independence, it has become the furniture capital of the Phillippines. Conde Nast named it one of the region's best island destinations. The city has almost a million inhabitants, the island almost two-and-a-half.

www.cebu.gov.ph/

TR3ATS GH, 785 V. Rama Ave, Cebu City; T:+63/324228881, *bemyguest@ tr3ats.com*; $9bed, Kitchen:N, B'fast:N, WiFi:Y, Pvt.room:Y, Locker:N, Recep:24/7; Note: luggage room, laundry, arpt trans, parking, a/c, new

Cebu Guesthouse, 211 Mango Ave, Cebu City; T:+63/322336010, *info@ cebuguesthouse.com/*; $9bed, Kitchen:Y, B'fast:$, WiFi:Y, Pvt.room:Y, Locker:Y, Recep:24/7; Note: resto/bar, central, nr ferry, tour desk, bikes, luggage rm, TV, a/c

LEGAZPI CITY is capital of Albay Province in the Bicol region, down the long winding island that it shares with Manila. It calls itself "City of Fun and

Adventure," which is a good idea. Lignon Hill Nature Park has good views of Mayon Volcano. Legazpi City Museum showcases the city's culture and history. Population is almost 200,000.

wowlegazpi.com/

Mayon Bpackers Hostel, #040 Brgy. 11 Maoyod, Legazpi City, Albay; *mayonbackpackers.wordpress.com/*, T:+63/0524800365, $7bed, Kitchen:Y, B'fast:Y, *mayonbackpackers@gmail.com;* WiFi:Y, Pvt.room:Y, Locker:Y, Recep:ltd; Note: luggage room, tea/coffee, parking, a/c, roof terrace, central, hard find

MANILA (inc, Mandaluyong City, Quezon City, Ermita, Makita, etc.) is one of the monster cities of Asia and the world, located on the eastern shores of Manila Bay and the western shores of Luzon Island. It is in fact *the* most densely populated city in the world, the city proper with more than a million-and-a-half people in an area only 38.5sq.km. Only its suburb Quezon City has more people, the two and fourteen others comprising Metro Manila, a conurbation of almost twelve million people and eleventh-largest in the world. The city is documented from the 10th century as the already Indianized and increasingly Islamicized — via Indonesia — trading kingdom of Maynila, with direct relations to China, also, playing rajahs off sultans off pirates and warlords.

The Spanish took advantage of the fragmented leadership, and made it the center of their Asian and Pacific activities in 1571. It was the hub of their galleon trade with Acapulco until 1898 when the Spanish left. Between 1899 and 1902, the Philippine–American War would result in the deaths of as many as 1.5 million Filipinos; Manila was the site of the bloodiest battle in the Pacific during WWII. Prosperity followed WWII, until dictator Ferdinand Marcos absconded with most of it. Corruption continually plagues the city's leadership, but little by little Manila is taking its place in the ranks of Asia's great cities.

Cultural institutions include Bahay Tsinoy, which documents Chinese contributions to the Philippines, the Intramuros Light and Sound Museum, the Metropolitan Museum of Manila, and the Museum of Manila. There are also the Museo Pambata, a children's museum, and the Museum of Philippine Political History, National Museum of the Philippines, the Plaza San Luis, the UST Museum of Arts and Sciences, and the DLS-CSB Museum of Contemporary Art and Design (MCAD). There are also numerous historic Catholic churches, and more than a few devoted to Muslims, Sikhs, Hindus, Buddhists, and Taoists. Major tourist destinations include the historic core of Intramuros, Chinatown, and the shopping and nightlife districts of Ermita and Malate. Don't forget to wear protection. There are many hostels, mostly for local "bed-spacers." There are also many converted flats, for tourists.

www.manila.gov.ph/

One Mackinson Place Dormtel, Road 3, Quezon City; T:029210541, *onemackinsonplace@yahoo.com*; $7bed, Kitchen:N, B'fast:N, WiFi:Y, Pvt.room:Y, *onemackinsonplace.com.ph/*, Locker:$, Recep:ltd; Note: hard to find, locals

Pinoy B'packers, Tivoli Garden Res, #2010/2011 Eugenia Tower, Coronado St, Hulo, Mandaluyong City

Pinoy B'packers, MC-T3 Dansalan Garden, 347 M. Vicen, Mandaluyong; T:025847623, *admin@   pinoybackpackers.com/*; $20bed, Kitchen:Y, B'fast:Y, WiFi:Y, Pvt.room:Y, Locker:Y, Recep:24/7; Note: pool, gym, a/c, TV, tea/ coffee

Rooms 498, 498 Boni Ave, Mandaluyong City; *roomsforrent.ph/*, T:+63/917235533, *inquiry@rooms498.com*; $12bed, Kitchen:Y, B'fast:N, WiFi:N, Pvt.room:N, Locker:N, Recep:ltd; Note: resto, laundry, parking

Crossroads Hostel, 76 Mariveles St, Highway Hills, Mandaluyong City; *crossroadshostel.wordpress.com/*, T:+63/9209595747, $13bed, Kitchen:Y, B'fast:Y, *crossroadshostel@gmail.com*, WiFi:Y, Pvt.room:N, Locker:Y; Note: laundry, tour desk, a/c, TV, mini-mkt, c.c. ok, luggage room

Happy Coconuts YH, 434 El Grande Ave, BF Homes, Sucat, Paranaque; *www.facebook.com/pages/Happy-Coconuts-Hostel*, T:+638288812

Manila Bay Hostel, #402, Bel-Air Apt, 1020 Roxas Blvd, Ermita, Manila; *www.facebook.com/pages/Manila-Bay-Hostel*, T:+63/23535814;

Green Mango Inn, 365 Aguirre Ave, BF Homes, Sucat, Parañaque City; *www.facebook.com/pages/Green-Mango-Inn*, T:+63/28208730, *gh_realty@yahoo.com*, $7bed, Kitchen:Y, B'fast:N, WiFi:Y, Pvt.room:Y, Locker:Y, Recep:24/7; Note: resto, luggage rm, prkng, lift, 14-day cancel

Where 2 Next, 1776 M. Adriatico St, Malate, Manila; *where2nexthostel.com/*, T:+63/23543533; $14bed, Kitchen:Y, B'fast:Y, WiFi:Y, Pvt.room:Y, Locker:Y, Recep:24/7; Note: resto/bar, maps, billiards, luggage rm, laundry, a/c, c.c. ok

Red Carabao, P Burgos St, Corner Kalayaan Ave, Makati, Manila; *facebook.com/RedCarabaoManila*, T:+63/27403211; $8bed, Kitchen:N, B'fast:Y, WiFi:Y, Pvt.room:N, Locker:Y, Recep:24/7; Note: billiards, luggage rm, laundry, a/c, bar

1 River Central, 1109 J.P. Rizal Guadalupe Viejo, Makati, Manila; *1rivercentral.com*, T:09178446366; $12bed, Kitchen:Y, B'fast:Y, WiFi:Y, Pvt.room:N, Locker:Y, Recep:24/7; Note: bikes, luggage rm, laundry, a/c, bar, safe deposit

Manila International YH, 4227 Tomas Claudio St, Baclaran, Parañaque; *hihostels.com/*, T:+63/28516934, *manilaintlyouthhostel@gmail.com*; $7bed, Kitchen:Y, B'fast:N, WiFi:Y, Pvt.room:N, Locker:N, Recep:ltd; Note: wh/chair ok, central

Our Melting Pot, 4/F Mavenue Bldg, Makati Ave cnr Guerrero St; *ourmeltingpot.hostel.com/*, T:+63/26595443; $15bed, Kitchen:Y, B'fast:Y, WiFi:Y, Pvt.room:Y, Locker:Y, Recep:24/7; Note: lift, forex, parking, luggage $, laundry, a/c, hard find

Friendly's Guesthouse, 1750 Adriatico St, Cnr Nakpil St, Malate; *friendlysguesthouse.com/*, T:024740742, *friendlysguesthouse@yahoo.com*; $9bed, Kitchen:Y, B'fast:N, WiFi:Y, Pvt.room:Y, Locker:Y, Recep:24/7; Note: wine/cheese nights, bar, tour desk

Islas8817 GH, 8817 San Juan St, San Antonio, Valley 2 Manila, PH; *islas8817.jimdo.com/*, T:+63/2829066, *islas8817@hotmail.co.jp*; $4bed, Kitchen:N,

B'fast:$, WiFi:Y, Pvt.room:Y, Locker:N, Recep:24/7; Note: wheelchair ok, resto, luggage rm, laundry, tour desk, a/c

MOALBAL is on a peninsula on the southwestern tip of Cebu, 55mi/89km from Cebu City. The island of Negros can be seen across the strait. It has a murky past of Muslim nomads and fantastic origin stories, but mostly it has a tourism industry based on diving and beaches. There are two beaches, Panagsama and White beach, with restos and bars.

www.moalboal.org.uk

Moalboal Backpacker Lodge, Panagsama Beach, Basdiot, Moalboal, PH; T:0324743053, *info@ moalboal-backpackerlodge.com/*; $7bed, Kitchen:Y, B'fast:N, WiFi:Y Pvt.room:N, Locker:Y, Recep:ltd; Note: luggage room, laundry, safe deposit, sea view

PUERTO GALERA is a town in the province of Oriental Mindoro, 80mi/130km south of Manila. It has some of the highest marine species diversity in the world. It is known for snorkeling and diving and has been called one of the most beautiful beaches in the world.

www.puertogalera.org/

Tuna Joe Backpackers, Sinandigan Beach, nr Sabang, Puerto Galera; *tunajoe.com/*, T:+63432873552, *tunajoebackpacker@yahoo.com*; $4bed, Kitchen:Y, B'fast:Y, WiFi:Y, Pvt.room:Y, Locker:Y, Recep:ltd; Note: pool, TV, bar, remote

PUERTO PRINCESA is a city of almost a quarter mil located on the western island of Palawan, for which it serves as capital. It has a rep as an Eco-Tourist resort center, clean and green, and is home to many beaches and resorts. The nearby Puerto Princesa Subterranean River National Park was named one of the New Seven Wonders of Nature. Tubbataha Reef is a UNESCO World Heritage Site, some 110mi/180km to the southeast.

www.puertoprincesaphilippines.com

Dallas Inn, 11 Carandang St, Puerto Princesa City; *dallasinnpalawan. com/*, T:+63/9199678558, *dallaspalawan@gmail.com*; $9bed, Kitchen:N, B'fast:N, WiFi:Y, Pvt.room:Y, Locker:Y, Recep:24/7; Note: luggage room, wh/chair ok, arpt trans, parking, tour desk

SAN FELIPE is a small city in the province of Zambales on the west coast of Luzon. It had the distinction of being buried in ash from Mt. Pinatubo a few years back.

The Circle Hostel, Sito Liwliwa, San Felipe Zambales; *facebook.com/ thecirclehostel/*, T:09178611929, *thecirclehostel@gmail.com*; $9bed, Kitchen:N, B'fast:Y, WiFi:Y, Pvt.room:N, Locker:Y, Recep:ltd; Note: bar, parking, midnight curfew, no lift, surfers

20) Sabah & Sarawak: East Malaysia (Borneo Island)

KOTA KINABULU is the capital of Sabah state in East Malaysia. With over a half million people in the greater metropolitan area, it is the largest urban centre in Borneo and the sixth largest in Malaysia. Originally inhabited by the local Bajau people, in the late 1800s the British North Borneo Company (BNBC) began to establish colonies. A railroad was built, a harbor was found, and business was conducted in rubber, rattan, honey, and wax based in the newly founded Jesselton, named after the company's Vice Chairman. These days, as capital of Sabah, commerce and industry are still prime movers of the economy, but tourism is growing. There is a Sunday market.

Kinabalu National Park, named for the mountain, not the city, is located about 90 kilometres from the city, and offers a way to beat the tropical rainforest heat. Nearby Keningau is popular for jungle trekking. Kota Kinabulu is also

home to the KK Jazz Festival. Other cultural venues include the Sabah State Museum, the Science and Technology Centre, Sabah Art Gallery, the Ethno Botanic Garden, and the Wisma Budaya Art Gallery. Monsopiad Cultural Village features cultural shows relating to the Kadazan-Dusun culture. That culture has been heavily impacted by Malay and other cultures introduced to the region, and the language is considered endangered. Better hurry to see traditional Borneo before it's gone. There are many hostels and the quality is good. The Indonesian side of the island has none. Languages are Malay, English, and tribal dialects. Currency is *ringgit* (MYR). Calling code is +60.
www.kotakinabalu.com

Stay-In Lodge, 1-4th Fl, Lot 121, Jl Gaya, Kota Kinabalu, Sabah; *stayinlodge.com/*, T:+6088272986, *stayinlodge@yahoo.com*; $7bed, Kitchen:N, B'fast:Y, WiFi:Y, Pvt.room:Y, Locker:N, Recep:24/7; Note: central, laundry, luggage room, bar

Borneo Global B-packers, #29 Karamunsing Godown, Jl Karamunsing; *borneotourstravel.com/*, T:+6088270976, *borneogb@gmail.com*; $4bed, Kitchen:N, B'fast:Y, WiFi:Y, Pvt.room:Y, Locker:N, Recep:24/7; Note: Sat TV, bar, parking, tour desk, laundry, not central, basic, cheap

Rainforest Lodge, Lot 48 Ground & 1st Flr., Jalan Pantai, Kota Kinabalu; T:088258228, *info@ rainforestlodgekk.com/*; $12bed, Kitchen:N, B'fast:Y, WiFi:Y, Pvt.room:Y, Locker:Y, Recep:24/7; Note: central, resto/bar, parking, tour desk, luggage ok, noise, a/c, c.c. ok

Tempurung Seaside Lodge, Tempurung Village, Kota Kinabulu, Sabah; T:088773066, *info@ borneotempurung.com/*; $39bed, Kitchen:N, B'fast:Y, WiFi:Y, Pvt.room:Y, Locker:N, Recep:24/7; Note: meals inc, resto/bar, parking, tour desk, billiards, luggage rm, c.c. ok

Masada Backpacker, #9, 1st Fl, Jl Masjid Lama, Bandaran Berjaya KK, Sabah; *masadabackpacker.com/*, T:088238494; $12bed, Kitchen:Y, B'fast:Y, WiFi:Y, Pvt.room:Y, Locker:Y, Recep:24/7; Note: tour desk, parking, a/c, central, few windows, all-day brekkie

Xplorer Backpackers, 1st Fl, 106/108, Jl Gaya, Kota Kinabulu, Sabah; T:+60/88538780, *info@ xplobackpackers.com/*; $9bed, Kitchen:N, B'fast:Y, WiFi:N, Pvt.room:Y, Locker:Y, Recep:24/7; Note: shops, tour desk, a/c, luggage room, arpt pickup, balconies

Borneo Adventure Ctr/Lodge, #1 Kampung Air Satu, Jl Haji Yacub, KK; *borneoadventurecenter@yahoo.com*, T:+60/88241515; $7bed; Kitchen:Y, B'fast:Y, WiFi:Y, Pvt.room:Y, Locker:Y, Recep:24/7; Note: central, laundry, luggage room, a/c

Akinabalu YH, 133 Jalan Gaya, Pusat Bandar, Kota Kinabalu, Sabah; T:088272188, *info@ akinabaluyh.com/*; $9bed, Kitchen:N, B'fast:Y, WiFi:Y, Pvt. room:Y, Locker:Y, Recep:24/7; Note: tour desk, luggage room, laundry, a/c, central

Borneo Beachouse (B'packers), Jl Mat Salleh House #122, Tanjung Aru; *borneobeachouse.com/*, T:088218331, *borneobeachouse@gmail.com*; $7bed, Kitchen:Y, B'fast:N, WiFi:Y, Pvt.room:Y, Locker:N, Recep:ltd; Note: parking, tour desk, laundry, luggage rm, c.c. ok, walk>arpt, beach

Travellers' Light B/P Lodge, Lot 19, Lorong Dewan (Australia Pl), KK, Sabah; *travellerslight.com/*, T:(6)088238877, *tvlodge@live.com*; $10bed, Kitchen:N, B'fast:Y, WiFi:Y, Pvt.room:Y, Locker:N, Recep:24/7; Note: central, nature garden, forex, tour desk, luggage room, a/c, c.c. ok

Borneo Backpackers, 24 Lorong Dewan, Kota Kinabulu, Sabah; T:088234009, *info@ borneobackpackers.com/*; $8bed, Kitchen:Y, B'fast:Y, WiFi:Y, Pvt.room:Y, Locker:Y, Recep:ltd; Note: central, restaurant, laundry, luggage room, a/c, c.c. ok, roofbar

Summer Lodge, 120 Jalan Gaya, Pusat Bandar, Kota Kinabulu, Sabah; *summerlodge.com/*, T:088244499, *summerlodgekk@yahoo.com*; $8bed, Kitchen:N, B'fast:Y, WiFi:Y, Pvt.room:Y, Locker:Y, Recep:ltd; Note: bar, tour desk, laundry, luggage room, arpt p-u, a/c, central

Step-in Lodge, Lot 1 Block L, Sinsuran Complex, Jl Tun Fuad Stephens, KK; T:088270071, *info@ stepinlodge.com/*, $9bed, Kitchen:Y, B'fast:Y, WiFi:Y,

Pvt.room:Y, Locker:Y, Recep:24/7; Note: central, parking, tour desk, laundry, luggage room, a/c, nite mkt

Bunibon Lodge, Lot 21, Lorong Dewan, (Aus. Pl.), Kota Kinabalu, Sabah; *bunibonlodge.com/*, T:+6088210801, *bunibonlodge@ymail.com*; $9bed, Kitchen:Y, B'fast:Y, WiFi:Y, Pvt.room:Y, Locker:Y, Recep:24/7; Note: tour desk, parking, laundry, a/c, central

Lavender Lodge, 6 Jalan Laiman Diki, Pusat Bandar, Kota Kinabulu, Sabah; *lavenderlodge.com.my*, T:088217119, *lavend07@streamyx.com*; $10bed, Kitchen:N, B'fast:Y, WiFi:Y, Pvt.room:Y, Locker:Y, Recep:24/7; Note: tour desk, parking, laundry, a/c, central

D'villa Rina Ria Lodge, km 53 Jl. Tinompok, Kundasang, Ranau, KK, Sabah; T:(6088)889282, *info@ dvillalodge.com.my/*; $10bed, Kitchen:Y, B'fast:Y, WiFi:Y, Pvt.room:Y, Locker:N, Recep:24/7; Note: 500m>Kinabalu Park, 1.5hr>KK, resto, tour desk, pkng, laundry

North Borneo Cabin, 74 Jl Gaya, Pusat Bandar, Kota Kinabalu, Sabah; T:088272800, *info@ northborneocabin.com/*; $7bed, Kitchen:Y, B'fast:Y, WiFi:Y, Pvt.room:N, Locker:N, Recep:24/7; Note: tour desk, luggage room, central

Borneo Gaya Lodge, 78 Jalan Gaya, Pusat Bandar, Kota Kinabalu, Sabah;, T:0178178765, *info@ borneogayalodge.com/*; $9bed, Kitchen:Y, B'fast:Y, WiFi:Y, Pvt.room:Y, Locker:N, Recep:24/7; Note: tour desk, laundry, luggage $, central, TV

KUCHING has approximately one million people and is the largest city and capital of the Malaysian state of Sarawak. It came into existence in 1841 as the private fiefdom of the British adventurer James Brooke as a reward for his arbitration on a dispute between local tribes and the sultan of Brunei. At that time, and for a long time, Sarawak was a city, and no more, before gradually expanding into its current size. Brooke immediately banned headhunting and began modernization of the city. This latter-day principality was ceded to the British government after three years of Japanese occupation and the end of WWII.

Historical sights include the former Astana palace of the White Rajahs (now Governor Palace of Sarawak), Fort Margherita, and the Tua Pek Kong temple. For shopping there's the Main Bazaar, India Street, and Chinatown. Natural attractions include Bako National Park, Kuching Wetlands National Park, Semenggoh Wildlife Center and orangutan orphanage, the Gunung Gading National Park and the Kubah National Park. There are numerous beach resorts and a cultural village, but my favorite is the Rainforest World Music Festival. Hostels are varied and good. C U there.
kuching.outer-court.com/

Berambih Lodge, No. 104 Ewe Hai St, Kuching, Sarawak; *budgetlodgekuching.com/*, T:082238589, *berambih_lodge@hotmail.com*; $7bed, Kitchen:N, B'fast:Y, WiFi:Y, Pvt.room:Y, Locker:N, Recep:24/7; Note: resto/bar, travel desk, luggage room, a/c, close to waterfront

Nomad Borneo B&B, 3 Jalan Green Hill, Kuching, Sarawak; T:082237831, *info@ borneobnb.com/*; $7bed, Kitchen:Y, B'fast:Y, WiFi:Y, Pvt.room:Y, Locker:Y, Recep:24/7; Note: resto/bar, tour desk, parking, luggage room, laundry, games

Beds GH, 229 Lot 91 Sec 50, Lorong 9, Jl Padungan, Kuching, Sarawak; T:082424229, *enquiry@ bedsguesthouse.com/*; $11bed, Kitchen:Y, B'fast:Y, WiFi:N, Pvt.room:Y, Locker:N, Recep:24/7; Note: bar, parking, tour desk, luggage room, laundry, a/c, not central

Lodge 121, Lot 121, 1st Fl, Sec 33 KTLD, Tabuan Rd, Kuching; T:082428121, *enquiry@ lodge121.com/*, $8bed, Kitchen:Y, B'fast:Y, WiFi:Y, Pvt.room:Y, Locker:Y, Recep:24/7, Note: tour desk, forex, parking, games, luggage room, a/c, near center

Wo Jia Lodge, 17 Jl Main Bazaar, Kuching, Sarawak; *wojialodge.com/*, T:082251776, *wojialodge@gmail.com*, $7bed, Kitchen:Y, B'fast:Y, WiFi:Y, Pvt.room:Y, Locker:N, Recep:24/7; Note: central, on waterfront nr bus, bar, tour desk, a/c

Threehouse B&B, 51 Upper China St, Kuching, Sarawak; *threehousebnb.com/*, T:+60/82423499, *threehousebnb@gmail.com*; $8bed, Kitchen:Y, B'fast:Y,

WiFi:Y, Pvt.room:Y, Locker:Y, Recep:24/7; Note: Chinatown, laundry, luggage room, parking, a/c, no windows

Tracks B&B, 1ˢᵗ Fl, #5, Jalan Greenhill, Kuching, Sarawak; T:+60/196407372, *enquiry@ tracksbnb.com/*; $8bed, Kitchen:Y, B'fast:Y, WiFi:Y, Pvt.room:Y, Locker:Y, Recep:24/7; Note: laundry, luggage room, a/c, central

Kuching Waterfront Lodge, #15 Main Bazaar, Kuching, Sarawak; *kuchingwaterftlodge.comron/*, T:082231111; $12bed, Kitchen:N, B'fast:Y, Wi-Fi:Y, Pvt.room:Y, Locker:Y, Recep:24/7; Note: a/c, c.c. ok, luggage room, waterfront

Mr. D's B&B, #26 Carpenter St, (China Town), Kuching, Sarawak; T:+60/82248852, *enquiry@ misterdbnb.com/*; $7bed, Kitchen:N, B'fast:Y, WiFi:Y, Pvt.room:Y, Locker:Y, Recep:24/7; Note: laundry, a/c, no windows in rooms

LABUAN is a federal territory in East Malaysia, located off the coast of the state of Sabah, and made up of Labuan Island and six smaller islands. It, too, was formerly ruled by the White Rajah James Brooke, before the Japanese occupied the island during WWII. For such a small area, it has a surprisingly varied and prosperous economy: offshore finance center, offshore oil and gas supply hub, and scuba diving. Popular dive sites are the Cement wreck, the American wreck, the Australian wreck and the Blue Water wreck. There are ferries to both Sabah and Brunei.

www.labuantourism.gov.my

Labuan Backpacker, Sabah, Labuan; *labuanbackpacker.blogg.se*, T:0168030868, *unclejackbackpacker@yahoo.com*; $7bed, Kitchen:N, B'fast:Y, WiFi:Y, Pvt.room:N, Locker:N, Recep:ltd; Note: bar, parking, a/c, nr ferry terminal

Siang GH, Lazenda 1, Jl Rancha Rancha 3.5km, Labuan, Malaysia; *siangguesthouse.com/*, T:+60/138162198, *bstlbn@streammyx.co*; $10bed, Kitchen:Y, B'fast:Y, WiFi:Y, Pvt.room:Y, Locker:Y, Recep:ltd; Note: tour desk, parking, laundry, luggage room, a/c, arpt p-u, Sat TV

MIRI is the second-largest city in the state of Sarawak, on the island of Borneo, and is the home of the Malaysian oil industry. The first oil well was drilled in 1910 and is now a state monument. Tourism is based on eco-tourism and four national parks: Mount Mulu, Niah, Lambir Hills, and Loagan Bunut. In addition there is the Lian Hua San Taoist temple and some killer beaches and coral reefs. Sounds like a gas... and oil.
www.journeymalaysia.com/MC_miri.htm

Minda Guesthouse, 1st-2nd Fl, Lot 637, North Yu Seng Road, Miri, Sarawak; T:085411422, *info@ mindaguesthouse.com/*; $7bed, Kitchen:N, B'fast:Y, WiFi:Y, Pvt.room:N, Locker:Y, Recep:ltd; Note: tour desk, game room, a/c, brekkie at 8

Tree Tops Lodge, Lot #210, Kampong Siwa Jaya, Bakam, Miri, Sarawak; *treetops-borneo.com/*, T:+60/85472172; $10bed, Kitchen:N, B'fast:Y, WiFi:Y, Pvt. room:Y, Locker:N, Recep:ltd; Note: restaurant, parking, pool, luggage room, 20k>town, Brunei bus

Miritrail GH, Sub Lot 10634, 1st-2nd Fl, Arpt Commercial Centre Miri; *miritrailguesthouse.com/*, T:+60/178503666, *miritrail@yahoo.com*; $9bed, Kitchen:N, B'fast:Y, WiFi:Y, Pvt.room:Y, Locker:N, Recep:ltd; Note: tour desk, a/c, nr arpt

SANDAKAN is the second-largest city in Sabah, East Malaysia, on the north-eastern coast of Borneo. It is known as the base for ecotourism in Sabah, including the Sepilok Orang Utan Rehabilitation Centre, the Rainforest Discovery Centre, Turtle Islands Park, Kinabatangan River and Gomantong Caves. It is also known for the Sandakan Death Marches, a series of forced marches in Borneo which resulted in the deaths of more than 3,600 Indonesian civilian slave labourers and 2,400 Allied prisoners of war held captive by the Empire of Japan. Other sights and landmarks include the Agnes Keith House, the Sandakan War Memorial Park, the Japanese Cemetery, the Puu Jih Shih Buddhist Temple, and Sam Sing Kung Temple. Kampung Buli Sim Sim is a stilt fishing village on the original site of Sandakan town. Sandakan Market is a good place to shop.
www.sabahtourism.com/

Harbourside Backpackers, Lot 43, 1ˢᵗ Fl, Block HS-4, Sandakan; *harboursidebackpackers.com/*, T:+6089217072; $8bed, Kitchen:Y, B'fast:Y, WiFi:Y, Pvt.room:Y, Locker:Y, Recep:ltd; Note: tour desk, forex, luggage room, laundry, a/c

Winho Lodge B&B, Lot 8 & 9, Block 19, 1ˢᵗ-2ⁿᵈ, Jalan Dua, Sandakan; *winholodge.com/*, T:+6089212310, *winholodge@gmail.com*; $9bed, Kitchen:Y, B'fast:Y, WiFi:Y, Pvt.room:Y, Locker:N, Recep:24/7; Note: tour desk, luggage room, laundry, a/c

Paganakandii Tropical Retreat, Mile 14, Jl Labuk, Sepilok; T:0128851005, *info@ paganakandii.com/*; $10bed, Kitchen:N, B'fast:Y, WiFi:N, Pvt.room:Y, Locker:N, Recep:ltd; Note: resto/bar, tour desk, parking, orangutans, laundry, a/c, basic, shuttle

Seaview Sandakan Hotel, Lot 126, 1ˢᵗ Fl, Jl Dua, Harbour Sq 14, Sandakan; *seaviewsandakan.com/*, T:089221221, *seaviewsandakan@yahoo.com*; $7bed, Kitchen:Y, B'fast:Y, WiFi:Y, Pvt.room:Y, Locker:N, Recep:ltd; Note: bike rent, tour desk, forex, ATM, TV, laundry, a/c, pancakes!

Sandakan Backpackers, Lot 108, Blk SH-11, Sandakan; T:0128323031, *sales@ sandakanbackpackers.com/*; $9bed, Kitchen:Y, B'fast:Y, WiFi:Y, Pvt.room:Y, Locker:N, Recep:24/7; Note: tour desk, luggage room, billiards, a/c, basic

21) Samoa

Samoa is divided into two parts: the US territory and the independent (formerly "West") Samoa, which have been divided for more than a hundred years, though the West has only been independent since 1962, when it separated from its colonial master New Zealand, the first Pacific Island nation to do so. The islands now known as 'Samoa' were likely settled about 3000 years ago by seafaring groups associated with the Lapita pottery-producing culture. Europeans came into the picture in the 18ᵗʰ century and began their cultural incursions in earnest with British missionaries in 1830. Apparently they weren't fond of the locals' predilection for headhunting. Other countries soon showed interest in the commercial possiblities here, including, Germany, France, and the US.

Soon there began a proxy civil war in which the colonial powers backed local combatants to further their own interests. This continued off and on for decades until the partition in 1899 between US eastern and German western Samoa. During WWI New Zealand intervened on behalf of Great Britain to administer the German half, and stayed on under League of Nations mandate. Incidents followed of harsh treatment, and resistance grew, until final independence in 1962. The traditional way of life is still important, including dancing, tattoos and kava drinking. In villages traditional open *fale* houses are common. Long exposure to European culture has yielded many artists, filmmakers and writers fluent in those media, plus massive adoption of hiphop culture as a symbol of rebellious youth, and café culture as a symbol of hip young adulthood. Rugby is big. The tourist industry is miniscule but growing. Need adventure? Language is Samoan and English, currency is the *tala* (WST), and calling code is +685.

www.samoa.travel/

APIA is the capital and only city in independent Samoa, with a population of almost 38,000 out of a total of some 180,000 in the entire country. It is the country's major port, also, and ferries serve Tokelau and Pago Pago in American Samoa. Fish and coconut meat are the main exports.

Pasefika Inn, PO Box 6114, Matautu-uta, Apia, Samoa; T:+685/20084, *info@ pasefikainn.ws/*; $30bed, Kitchen:N, B'fast:Y, WiFi:Y, Pvt.room:Y, Locker:N, Recep:24/7; Note: parking, a/c, luggage room, pool

Tatiana Motel, P.O. Box 230, Apia, Samoa; *tatiana-motel.com/*, T:+685/26829, *tatiana.motel@lesamoa.net*; $17bed, Kitchen:N, B'fast:Y, WiFi:Y, Pvt.room:Y, Locker:N, Recep:ltd; Note: basic, central

Outrigger Hotel, Motootua, On the Cross, Island Road, Apia, Samoa; *samoanoutriggerhotel.com/*, T:+685/20042, *outrigger@samoa.ws*; $31bed,

Kitchen:Y, B'fast:Y, WiFi:Y, Pvt.room:Y, Locker:Y, Recep:ltd; Note: resto/bar, laundry, luggage ok, a/c, c.c. ok, pool, 15 min walk>town

22) Timor L'este

Timor is an island in the easternmost of the Lesser Sunda Islands, comprised of an original Melanesian/Papuan population and long fought over between the Dutch and Portuguese colonialists. Timor L'este (East Timor, Timor Timur in Indonesian) is the former Portuguese colony that was snatched by Indonesia when the Portuguese withdrew after a military coup in the early 1970's. They fought a guerrilla war until 1999 when a referendum was held and independence declared. The Indonesian torched the place on departure and the UN governed until the small impoverished country could stand on its own. There are excellent weavings on both sides of the island, more reminiscent of Guatemala than Sumatra. Tetum, Portuguese, Indonesian, and English are spoken. Calling code is +670.

DILI is a city of a couple hundred thou and the capital of Timor L'este. Though heavily damaged in the final days of Indonesian rule, there are some vestiges of the previous Portuguese colony.
www.timor.org/

Dili Beach Hotel, Pantai Kelapa, Beach Road, Dili, Timor-Leste; *dilibeachhotel.com/*, T:+670/3310493; $20Bed, Pvt.room:Y, Kitchen:N, B'fast:Y, WiFi:Y, Locker:N, Recep:ltd; Note: resto/bar, pool, pizza, ex-pats, luggage room, tour desk

23) Tonga

TONGA is a kingdom and the only Pacific island nation to have never been officially colonized. Over 50 of its 172 islands are inhabited. It would appear to have been first settled around 1000BCE by the proto-Polynesian Lapita culture and long in close contact with Samoans and possibly others elsewhere. The Dutch were the first Europeans to show up in 1616, and James Cook made his first trip in 1773. The British soon began missionary work and by 1900 had gotten the locals to enter into an agreement of protection within the Empire, though it never gave up its monarchy, which has been continuous throughout.

Though it functions as a constitutional monarchy, all too often the monarchy outweighs the constitution and little dissent is tolerated. That the monarchy controls key services and dallies in get-rich-quick schemes while much of the country wallows in poverty has been a cause of protests, rioting, and even deaths. Tourism is poorly developed, and most people depend on remittances from overseas family members that number as many as the population in-country. Still, if you're self-motivated and and a DIY-er, a visit to Tonga can be rewarding. People wear grass skirts to church on Sundays and the graveyard quilt art must be seen. As elsewhere in Polynesia, obesity is rampant. Tongan and English are the languages, Pa'anga (TOP) the currency, and +676 the calling code.

www.thekingdomoftonga.com

NEIAFU is a town of 6000, second-largest in the kingdom of Tonga.

Three Little Birds GH, Toula Village, Vavau, Neiafu, Tonga; T:+676/8630424, *threelittlebirdsguesthouse@gmail.com*; $21Bed, Pvt.room:Y, Kitchen:Y, B'fast:Y, *threelittlebirdsguesthouse.com/*, WiFi:Y, Locker:N, Recep:ltd; Note: arpt trans free, resto/bar, bikes, parking, laundry,

TONGATAPU is the main island of Tonga, with over 70,000 of its 100,000 population, of which over 20,000 reside in the capital of Nuku'alofa. There are lagoons and coral reefs and important breeding grounds for birds and fish. There are archeological ruins. There are even a couple decent bars in downtown Nuku'alofa that attract both locals and foreigners, and where safety is not a big issue; that's rare. What there are NOT a lot of, are sandy beaches, oh well. The place shuts down on Sunday.

Toni's Guesthouse, Tofoakoloua Tongatapu, Tonga; *tonisguesthouse.com/*, T:+676/7748720, *tonigh2@yahoo.co.uk*; $9bed, Kitchen:Y, B'fast:N, WiFi:Y, Pvt. room:Y, Locker:N, Recep:24/7; Note: kava nights, parking, laundry, luggage ok, tours $, far from town

Nukualofa-Tonga World, Wellington Rd, Kolomotua, Nukualofa; *hihostels.com/*, T:+676/8747282, *mtaka@whats-wa.com*; $22bed, Kitchen:Y, B'fast:N, WiFi:Y, Pvt.room:N, Locker:Y, Recep:ltd; Note: wheelchair ok, forex, luggage room, laundry, tour desk, c.c. ok

24) Vanuatu

VANUATU is a Melanesian country located some 1090mi/1750km east of Cairns, north Australia, maybe half that distance west of Fiji, and home to over 220,000 people. The first Austronesian-speaking people were here by at least 4000 years ago, and Papuan-like aboriginals possibly much earlier, if my theories are correct. The Iberians—Portuguese working for the Spanish— showed up in 1606, thinking it was the legendary Australia. It was a false start, though, and the French then English finally returned in the late 1700's to the renamed New Hebrides. The discovery of sandalwood provoked a rash of immigrants from 1825-30, many of whom by 1860 were being 'blackbirded' to do slave labor elsewhere. Britain and France ruled jointly until WWII.

Then one of the strangest phenomena in human history occurred, the emergence of 'cargo cults,' wherein true believers would pray and beseech— and build runways—for their gods to deliver industrial products to them. If that's not weird enough already, the messiah's name was John Frum. The religion still exists today. The country became independent in 1980. Agriculture and tourism are the two main industries, scuba diving one of the main attractions. Almost every family grows at least some of their own food, and music is still a major manifestation of the culture. English, French and Bislama (pidgin) are the main languages, *vatu* the currency, and +678 the calling code.

vanuatu.travel/

PORT VILA is the capital and largest city of Vanuatu, with more than 44,000 inhabitants. It gets only a few more tourists than that every year. It's a beach.

www.portvilavanuatu.com/index.php

Coconut Palms Resort, Cornwall St, Seaside, Efate Port Vila, Vanuatu; T:+678/23696, sales@ *coconutpalms.vu/;* $55bed, Kitchen:N, B'fast:$, WiFi:Y, Pvt.room:Y, Locker:N, Recep:24/7; Note: resto/bar, parking, laundry, feast $, a/c, c.c. ok, tour desk, pool

Bluepango Motel, P.O. Box 4033, Port Vila, Vanuatu; *bluepango.com/,* T:+678/25285, *bluepango@hotmail.com;* $15bed, Kitchen:Y, B'fast:N, WiFi:Y, Pvt.room:Y, Locker:N, Recep:24/7; Note: pool, parking, laundry, a/c, beach, cats, kava bar next door

City Lodge, Lini (Kumul) Highway, Port Vila, Vanuatu; *citylodge.com.vu/,* T:+678/26826, *citylodge@vanuatu.com;* $20bed, Kitchen:Y, B'fast:N, WiFi:Y, Pvt.room:Y, Locker:N, Recep:24/7; Note: city center, parking, tour desk, a/c, c.c. ok, basic, hot

(ESPIRITU) SANTO is the big island of Vanuatu. It has a peak higher than 6000ft/1800mt, and its largest town Luganville has over 10,000 people. It was the site of many WWII battles, which started its wreck-diving tourist industry of today. Champagne Beach is popular.

Turtle Bay Resort, Turtle Bay, Santo, Vanuatu; T:+678/37988, *stay@ turtlebayresort.vu/;* $26bed, Kitchen:Y, B'fast:N, WiFi:Y, Pvt.room:Y, Locker:N, Recep:24/7; Note: resto/bar, parking, laundry, luggage ok, pool, tour desk, c.c. ok

About The Author

American ex-pat Hardie Karges took his first extended international trip at the age of twenty-one in 1975 and traveled to his first ten countries within two years, all for less than two thousand dollars. Thus began a way of life that has taken him to some 150 countries (and counting), living and working in a dozen of them, learning several languages and trading in folk art and cottage industry products. He has also published poetry and created videos, before finally deciding to write about what he knows best—travel. His first book, "Hypertravel: 100 Countries in 2 Years," was published in 2012. The full set of "Backpackers & Flashpackers" is projected to include eight to ten volumes and be completed in 2014.

If you would like more information, or to make an inquiry or just leave a comment, please visit our blog at *backpackers-flashpackers.net/* or our *BackpackersFlashpackers* page on FaceBook.

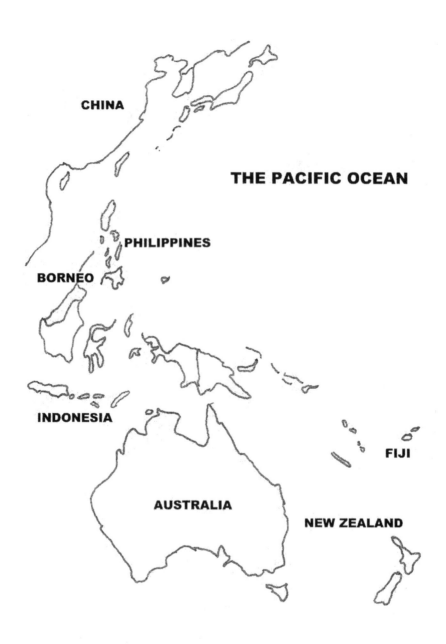

CHINA

THE PACIFIC OCEAN

PHILIPPINES

BORNEO

INDONESIA

FIJI

AUSTRALIA

NEW ZEALAND

4104711R00093

Printed in Great Britain
by Amazon.co.uk, Ltd.,
Marston Gate.